"Peter Martyr Vermigli is undoubtedly one of the most significant Reformed theologians of the sixteenth century and his *Common Places* is the crown jewel of his collected works. The rendering of this work into contemporary English is a great service to the understanding of Reformation thought and will be enriching for scholars and pastors alike. Vermigli's theological training and acumen are on full display here and the results are rightly esteemed as a masterwork of Reformed theology."

—JORDAN J. BALLOR

The Acton Institute, Junius Institute, author of Covenant, Causality, and Law: A Study in the Theology of Wolfgang Musculus

"With this precise but grandly readable translation, Reformation scholars owe a debt of gratitude to the editors and translator for this initial volume in this new series on Peter Martyr Vermigli's *Common Places*. Kirk Summers has faithfully and eloquently rendered Vermigli who is here at his subtle and forceful best; and has thus opened to a wider audience the Reformer's thought on some of the questions most central to the disputes of the sixteenth century: sin, human nature, what imputation entails, and even the nature of sacramental grace. Further, Summers's painstaking apparatus (Vermigli often quoted his sources from memory) lays bare Vermigli's vast command of the literature on these questions. Honor due."

—GARY JENKINS

Eastern University; author of Calvin's Tormentor's: Understanding the Conflicts that Shaped the Reformer

"Legend has it that Peter Martyr Vermigli descended out of the Italian Alps as the 'ready-made Reformer,' and his *Common Places* certainly confirm both his reputation and why so many esteemed his work. His *Common Places* were posthumously extracted from his biblical commentaries, which means that they are insightfully exegetical and theological. Students of the Reformation would do well to pick up this book and see for themselves the deep currents that run through his work. Students of Scripture will also greatly profit from one who knows the Bible so well."

—J. V. FESKO

Harriet Barbour Professor of Systematic and Historical Theology, Reformed Theological Seminary, Jackson, Mississippi

"In 1563, not long after the death of Peter Martyr Vermigli in Zurich, Theodore Beza urged on Heinrich Bullinger the need for a systematic theology to be compiled from Vermigli's immense corpus of scriptural commentary—"*eine Dogmatik in nuce.*" Owing in good part to Anthony Marten's Elizabethan translation, Vermigli's *Common Places* became one of the most influential of all Reformed systematic theologies, especially in the English-speaking world. Kirk Summers has made a selection of these commonplaces pertaining to the pivotal Christian teaching concerning Original Sin and rendered them into lucid, legible, modern English. For any scholar or aspiring theologian attuned to the Reformed tradition this volume should be obligatory reading."

—W.J. TORRANCE KIRBY

McGill University, author of The Zurich Connection and Tudor Political Theology

"According to Peter Martyr Vermigli, the supreme end and highest good in life is to be justified in Christ, accepted in love by the eternal Father. However, it is impossible to appreciate the significance of this acceptance until one has first grasped the catastrophic problem of original sin, the desolate pit from which God raises sinners to make them saints. In addition to answering critical questions surrounding the doctrine (i.e., What is sin? Who is responsible for it? And how does it spread?), this volume showcases Peter Martyr's convictions on a host of related topics including divine creation, humanity's *infidelitas*, total depravity, sexual relations, *imago Dei*, natural gifts, and the necessity of imputed righteousness as the basis for divine favor."

—CHRIS CASTALDO

Lead Pastor of New Covenant Church, Naperville., author of Justified in Christ: The Doctrines of Peter Martyr Vermigli and John Henry Newman

"Vermigli was one of the most important theologians of the sixteenth century. His *Loci Communes* is a collated summary of his theology and I am delighted to see this part of it made accessible in a new translation to an English speaking readership."

—DR. ROBERT LETHAM

Professor of Systematic & Historical Theology, Union School of Theology, Wales, UK

PETER MARTYR VERMIGLI
COMMON PLACES:

On Original Sin

PETER MARTYR VERMIGLI

COMMON PLACES:

ON ORIGINAL SIN

Translated and Edited by Kirk Summers

DAVENANT PRESS 2024

ISBN: 1-949716-35-X
ISBN-13: 978-1-949716-35-1

Cover design and Typesetting by
Rachel Rosales, Orange Peal Design

TABLE OF CONTENTS

FOREWORD AND
GENERAL INTRODUCTION

Chris Castaldo

Confronted by the persecution, force, and cruelty of this world, Peter Martyr Vermigli (1499–1562) urged Christians to leave the shadows of ignorance and recognize two realities: their identity in Christ and the sure hope of one day seeing God face to face.[1] This, he contends, is "man's ultimate happiness," the delight that surpasses all worldly pleasure—to be accepted by the eternal Father in Christ.[2]

In his earliest surviving work, his commentary on the Apostles' Creed (1541), Vermigli strikes this note, taking up the problem of ignorance among Christians concerning their salvation in Christ. The solution, he contends, is a diligent study of the faith that draws from the inspired text of Scripture, applying its redemptive insight to a range of theological, moral, and political challenges. Herein lies Vermigli's genius. As a biblical exegete and first-rate phi-

---

1. As in his *Credo*, Vermigli makes this point in his comments on Aristotle's *Nicomachean Ethics*. Peter Martyr Vermigli, *The Peter Martyr Reader*, ed. John Patrick Donnelly, Frank A. James III, and Joseph C. McLelland (Kirksville: Truman State University Press, 1999), 24–26, 99.

2. Vermigli, *Peter Martyr Reader*, 7, 51, 99.

losopher, he was able to connect divine truth to the most vexing questions of his day. And as a theologian he offered this reflection with an abiding concern for the Church's calling in the world. Such cross-disciplinary erudition emerged from his remarkable background.

In 1514, at age fifteen, Peter Martyr (as he became known) entered the Augustinian order in the town of Fiesole, nearly eight kilometers from his native Florence.[3] After three years, during which Vermigli distinguished himself as a precocious student, he was sent north to the monastery of San Giovanni di Verdara to begin studies at the University of Padua.

Founded in 1222, the University of Padua reached the apex of prestige in the opening years of the sixteenth century. There, the young Florentine encountered a rich tradition of Aristotle.[4] Without getting buried in hair-splitting partisanship that sometimes afflicted Aristotelian schools, Vermigli imbibed the Philosopher's logic and methodology. Meanwhile, his monastery provided a firm grounding in the study of Renaissance humanism.

Exceptionally focused, Vermigli supplemented his formal training with a rigorous course of private study—a

---

3. According to Simler's *Oratio*, Martyr's mother had taught him Latin when he was a child. Simler, "Oratio," in *Life, Letters, and Sermons*, trans. and ed. John Patrick Donnelly, The Peter Martyr Library, vol. 5 (Kirksville: Thomas Jefferson University Press, 1999), 11.

4. For a taxonomy of the various Aristotelian "schools" of the day, see John Patrick Donnelly, *Calvinism and Scholasticism in Vermigli's Doctrine of Man and Grace*, Studies in Medieval and Reformation Thought 18 (Leiden: Brill, 1976), 13–41; and Philip McNair, *Peter Martyr in Italy: An Anatomy of Apostasy* (Oxford: Clarendon, 1967), 86–115. Hereafter *PMI*.

routine that was aided by his monastery's exquisite library.[5] After finding numerous errors in the Latin translations of Aristotle, he proceeded to study Greek by night in order to read the sources. The acquisition of this language opened the door for Martyr to engage Renaissance humanism with greater depth and immediacy. Under the tutelage of Professor Pietro Bembo, arguably the most distinguished humanist scholar to be associated with San Giovanni di Verdara, Vermigli acquired an insatiable appetite for the study of classical texts.[6] After eight years in Padua, Martyr underwent priestly ordination and simultaneously received a doctorate in theology (1526).[7]

The seven years following Vermigli's departure from Padua opened new vocational horizons. He was elected to the office of public preacher, an illustrious position at the time. Martyr traveled through Northern Italy lecturing on Scripture and philosophy, and, whenever possible, he studied these subjects with careful attention.[8] In just a few years, while serving in Bologna, Vermigli also taught himself the Hebrew language—no small feat in those days—

---

5. McNair says, "This library was one of the great formative influences on Martyr's early years." *PMI*, 93.

6. The "ambience of [Padua's] devout and learned humanism" is described by Dermot Fenlon, *Heresy and Obedience in Tridentine Italy: Cardinal Pole and the Counter Reformation* (Cambridge: Cambridge University Press, 1972), 26.

7. Simler, "Oratio," in Vermigli, *Life, Letters, and Sermons*, 17.

8. According to Simler, such study would mostly happen in the houses of his Congregation at Padua, Ravenna, Bologna, and Vercelli. Simler, "Oratio," in Vermigli, *Life, Letters, and Sermons* 17.

with the assistance of a certain Jewish doctor named Isaac.[9] So distinguished did Vermigli's ministry become that his Augustinian order described him as *predicatorem eximium* (an exceptional preacher).[10] Then, in the spring of 1530, he was appointed vicar of the Augustinian house in Bologna. It was here, according to McNair, that Vermigli's preaching and teaching ministry led him toward a deeper and more intentional routine of biblical exegesis.

From the Schoolmen he turned to the Fathers, from the Fathers to the Vulgate, and from the Vulgate to the Source itself—the lively Oracles of God in their original expression. At Padua he had learned Greek to read Aristotle; at Bologna he learned Hebrew to read Scripture.[11]

As his name grew famous in the largest Italian cities, Vermigli was promoted to a higher position. By unanimous consent, he was made abbot of his order's monastery in Spoleto.[12] Effectively navigating the landmines of Spoleto's volatile politics, he managed to bring moral order out of chaos. Such vision and administrative skill distinguished Vermigli as capable of implementing reform, an ability that in turn earned him a new and larger role as abbot of San Pietro ad Aram in Naples.

Josiah Simler, Martyr's disciple and biographer, identifies Naples as the place where Vermigli's theological journey demonstrably turned a corner. During the three years

---

9. Simler, "Oratio," in Vermigli, *Life, Letters, and Sermons*, 17.

10. McNair, *PMI*, 118.

11. McNair, *PMI*, 124–25.

12. Spoleto is roughly 200 kilometers southeast of Florence, a little more than halfway to Rome.

of Peter Martyr's sojourn at San Pietro (1537–40), according to Simler, "the greater light of God's truth" began to shine upon him.[13] In McNair's analysis, this "greater light" was essentially "the doctrine of Justification by Faith alone…The acceptance of this vital doctrine entailed so drastic a reorientation of heart and mind that it amounted to conversion."[14]

With this new theological orientation, Vermigli moved north in May of 1541 to become prior of the prestigious monastery of San Frediano in the Republic of Lucca. It was there he initiated a series of educational and ecclesiastical reforms that have been likened to Calvin's work in Geneva. But after a mere fifteen months of such Gospel renewal, Pope Paul III hastened its demise by reinstituting the Roman Inquisition. Recognizing discretion as the better part of valor, Vermigli renounced his vows and made the difficult decision to flee his homeland.

It was Martin Bucer who arranged for Vermigli's academic appointment to the College of Saint Thomas in Strasbourg. The Italian exile was expected to teach sacred letters, which he proceeded to do from the Old Testament.

---

13. Simler, "Oratio," in Vermigli, *Life, Letters, and Sermons*, 19. Simler also notes that it was during his three years in Naples that Martyr "fell into a serious and deadly sickness," although we have no indication whether this experience factored into his conversion (22). This disease is thought to have been malaria.

14. McNair, *PMI*, 179. Frank James echoes this interpretation, in which he states, "There is little doubt that Simler understood this 'greater light of God's truth' to be the doctrine of justification by faith alone." "*De Iustificatione*: The Evolution of Peter Martyr Vermigli's Doctrine of Justification," Ph.D. diss., Westminster Theological Seminary, 2000, 1.

While in Strasbourg, Vermigli also married a former nun from Metz named Catherine Dammartin, "a lover of true religion," especially admired for her charity. After eight years of marriage, she died in February 1553, but Peter Martyr would marry again, another Katie, in May 1559.

Following five fruitful years of teaching in the Alsatian city, Vermigli received an invitation in 1547 from Archbishop Thomas Cranmer to fortify the newly independent Church of England with Reformed theology as Regius Chair of Divinity at Oxford. Among his many accomplishments in this period, he lectured on Romans, produced various theological treatises, championed Protestantism at the famous Eucharistic Disputation of 1549, and assisted Cranmer in reforming the Church of England by revising the Prayer Book, in the formulation of the Forty-Two Articles (later condensed to the authoritative Thirty-Nine Articles), and by contributing to the Reformation of Ecclesiastical Laws from 1551 to 1553.

With the accession of the Catholic Queen Mary in 1553, Vermigli was forced to flee England. Returning to Strasbourg, he was immediately restored to his position at the Senior School. And in addition to teaching and writing theological works, he gathered with Marian exiles in his home to study and pray. Eventually, he accepted Heinrich Bullinger's offer in 1556 to succeed Conrad Pellican at the Academy of Zurich.

Despite numerous opportunities to lecture throughout Europe, including invitations from Calvin to teach in Geneva and pastor the Italian congregation, Peter Martyr remained in Zurich. The exception was his journey to the Colloquy of Poissy with Theodore Beza in 1561, where he debated Catholic leaders before the French Crown and witnessed to Queen Catherine de' Medici in their native Italian.

Vermigli died in Zurich on November 12, 1562, in the presence of his wife and friends. According to Simler, who was present along with Heinrich Bullinger and a small group of others: "[Peter Martyr] was silent in deep personal reflection; then he turned to us and stated with a rather clear voice that he acknowledged life and salvation in Christ alone, who had been given by the Father to the human race as its only savior." This catchphrase "salvation in Christ alone" aptly summarizes Vermigli's doctrine, a faith in which he lived and died.

Vermigli's *Loci Communes*

Exposure to Vermigli as a theologian often begins with reading his *scholia* or *topoi* (treatments of various "topics"), which appear throughout his biblical commentaries and which Robert Masson gathered and published in London as the *Loci Communes* ("Common Places") in 1576.[15] The *loci* method, which was experiencing a revival in Martyr's day, might be likened to a surgical procedure for its rela-

---

15. Also known as Robert le Maçon, Sieur de la Fontaine, Masson was minister of the French congregation in London. Personally familiar with Peter Martyr's work in England, he also attended the Poissy conference in 1562. For the structuring of Vermigli's *Loci Communes*, Masson used John Calvin's *Institutes* as a model, arranging the topics in four books, an understandable decision given the theological solidarity shared by the Italian and French theologians, not to mention the desire to offer a unified presentation of Reformed doctrine. The scope and sequence of the work are familiar: God the Creator; sin and salvation; predestination; calling; union with Christ; resurrection; Holy Spirit; Church; sacraments; magistrates and state.

tively narrow scope and meticulous analysis of a subject.[16] More than any other figure, Aristotle (384–22 BC) is credited for having popularized the approach, followed by Cicero (106–43 BC), who had himself first encountered it in the Philosopher's *Topica*.[17] The method also drew from the humanist tradition represented by the likes of Lorenzo Valla (1407–57), with its trenchant historical, grammatical, and rhetorical analysis.[18] In Vermigli's context, the writing of theological *loci* often amalgamated these dialectical and rhetorical methods.[19] With regard to the former, it was a way to systematically focus argumentation by granting, denying, and admitting proof (*concedo, nego, admitto casum*). Concerning the latter, it applied the tools of exegesis to texts.

---

16. For an overview of its history and development, see Joseph C. McLelland, "A Literary History of the Loci Communes," in *A Companion to Peter Martyr Vermigli*, ed. W. J. Torrance Kirby, Emidio Campi, and Frank A. James III (Leiden: Brill, 2009), 479–94.

17. The *Topica* of Aristotle is part of his *Organon*, a collection of logical works addressing principles and methods of presenting evidence.

18. Cesare Vasoli, "Loci Communes and the Rhetorical and Dialetical Traditions," In *Peter Martyr Vermigli and Italian Reform*, ed. Joseph C. McLelland (Waterloo, Ontario: Wilfred Laurier University Press, 1980), 20–21.

19. Paul Oskar Kristeller, *Renaissance Thought: The Classic, Scholastic and Humanist Strains* (New York: Harper & Row, 1961), 92–119. This was the case, for instance, at institutions featuring a mixture of scholastic and humanist curricula, such as the University of Padua, where Vermigli received his education, or Heidelberg University, from which Martin Bucer was influenced during his study at the Dominican monastery in Heidelberg. See Martin Greschat, *Martin Bucer: A Reformer and His Times* (Louisville: Westminster John Knox Press, 2004), 18–20.

Published some fourteen years after his death, Vermigli's *Loci Communes* would become one of the most significant theological works of the later sixteenth century. Joseph McLelland has offered a literary history of the *Loci*, explaining that it was natural for Peter Martyr's disciples to gather various *scholia* together into a theological compendium as a way to elucidate his thought.[20] In time, Vermigli's *Loci Communes* would see over a dozen editions following its initial publication in 1576 and become a central vehicle for spreading Reformed theology throughout Europe and beyond.[21] "The English translation of 1583 held special place," writes McLelland, "traveling to the New World in good condition. In a recent lecture at Harvard, Diarmaid MacCulloch stated: 'the works of Peter Martyr were turned into a sort of themed theological textbook, *The Commonplaces*. If you looked into the library here

---

20. Some of these *scholia* were relatively brief, no more than a paragraph. Others are lengthy treatises. As early as 1563, the year after Vermigli's death, Theodore Beza wrote a letter dated July 1, 1563, urging Heinrich Bullinger to consider a systematic theology from Peter Martyr's writings. McLelland, "A Literary History," 486.

21. The English translation of the *Loci Communes* was produced by Anthony Marten (d. 1597), who used Masson's version as the foundation. He slightly modified the arrangement of topics and added new material, particularly the large appendix that essentially comprises Book Five. His title was *The Common Places of the most famous and renowned Divine Doctor Peter Martyr, divided into four principal parts, with a large addition of many theological and necessary discourses, some never extant before. Translated and partly gathered by Anthony Marten, one of the Sewers of her Majesty's most Honorable Chamber* (London: H. Denham and H. Middleton, 1583).

at Harvard in 1636, I suspect that would be [the] most thumbed book you would find."[22]

In reading Vermigli's *Loci Communes*, one might wonder: *Was he more of a humanist or scholastic?* Peter Martyr's trenchant work in philology, patristics, exegesis, and rabbinical studies suggests the former, whereas his reliance on four-fold causality (distinguishing between *substantia* and *accidentia*, and the *quaestio*) and use of natural metaphors might suggest the latter. In truth, Vermigli was shaped by both elements of his remarkable background. Born in Florence—capital of the Italian Renaissance—and formed at the University of Padua, a center of Aristotelian philosophy and scholasticism, Peter Martyr employed both traditions in combating theological ignorance.[23]

Some five hundred years later, the shadows of ignorance continue to recede, and Peter Martyr's *Loci Communes* continues to speak, imparting illumination to those who will follow the example of Vermigli's ancient mentor, Augustine: *tolle lege, tolle lege* ("take up and read, take up and read").

---

22. McLelland, "A Literary History," 488, citing Diarmaid MacCulloch, "Can the English Think for Themselves? The Roots of the English Reformation," *Harvard Divinity Bulletin* 30, no. 1 (Spring 2001), 19.

23. Joseph C. McLelland, "Peter Martyr Vermigli: Scholastic or Humanist?" in *Peter Martyr Vermigli and Italian Reform*, ed. Joseph C. McLelland (Waterloo, Ontario: Wilfrid Laurier University Press, 1980), 141.

VOLUME INTRODUCTION

Kirk Summers

The beginning of Peter Martyr Vermigli's (1499–1562) second book of the *Common Places* examines the core question of mankind's standing before God: In what way did the sin and fall of Adam accrue to the guilt of his posterity and subject all people to death?[1] The Church traditionally held the view that the first sin of Adam, wherein Eve induced him to eat the forbidden fruit, had catastrophic ramifications for the human race.[2] Because he stood as the

---

1. For another overview of Vermigli's views on original sin focused more on his scholastic methodology, see John Patrick Donnelly, SJ, *Calvinism and Scholasticism in Vermigli's Doctrine of Man and Grace* (Leiden: Brill, 1976), 104–16. For a briefer overview of the sources for the first section taken from the Genesis commentary, see Emidio Campi, "Genesis Commentary: Interpreting Creation," in *A Companion to Peter Martyr Vermigli*, ed. Torrance Kirby, Emidio Campi, and Frank James III (Leiden: Brill, 2009), 209–30, esp. 225–26.

2. The classic treatment of the history of the doctrine can be found in Julius Gross, *Geschichte des Erbsündendogmas: Ein Beitrag zur Geschichte des Problems vom Ursprung des Übels*, 4 vols. (Munich: Ernst Reinhardt Verlag, 1960–72). The first volume covers the period from the time of the Bible to Augustine; the second deals with the developments from Augustine to the early Scholastic period; the third looks at the developments in the late Scholastic period (twelfth through

representative head of humanity, his rebellious act against God, the original sin, warranted death for all who issued forth from him. He "held in his loins" the entire human race. Thus, every infant who comes into the world bears the stain of this sin and thus deserves eternal damnation. God in his grace, however, has provided a remedy for this dilemma, first through baptism as a seal, but ultimately through the sacrifice of his Son Jesus Christ.

Vermigli's presentation of the doctrine of original sin falls within the broad spectrum of this traditional orthodox position. The common opponents of all, be they Roman Catholic or Protestant, were the old Pelagian heretics from the time of Augustine (354–430) and their contemporary heir as represented in the figure of Albert Pighius (c. 1490–1542).[3] The latter attended the Colloquy of Re-

---

fifteenth centuries); the fourth encompasses the Reformation and beyond. For a perceptive analysis of Calvin's views, see Barbara Pitkin, "Nothing but Concupiscence: Calvin's Understanding of Sin and the *Via Augustini*," *Calvin Theological Journal* 34 (1999): 347–69; and Nico Vorster, "Calvin's Modification of Augustine's Doctrine of Original Sin," in *Restoration through Redemption: John Calvin Revisited*, ed. Henk Belt (Leiden: Brill, 2013), 45–61.

3. Pelagius lived from 360 to 418. At the prompting of Augustine, Pope Innocent I condemned him, primarily because of his views on the impact of the Fall on man's free will. Pelagius believed that human beings retain their power to choose good or evil even post-Fall, while rejecting the notion of inherited sin. His student Coelestius (or Celestius, precise dates unknown) pushed his teachings to their extremes, causing alarm among Christian leadership. The Council of Ephesus of 431 condemned his teachings as heresy. See Robert Evans, *Pelagius: Inquiries and Reappraisals* (New York: The Seabury Press, 1968); and Brinley Rees, *Pelagius: A Reluctant Heretic* (Wolfeboro, NH: The Boydell Press, 1988).

gensburg (1541) on the Catholic side and remained loyal to the papacy for his entire life despite certain doctrinal differences. Throughout this section of the *Loci*, therefore, these two serve as the foils against which Vermigli makes his presentation. He structures his arguments in good dialectic fashion by stating the opposing views and contradictions and then resolving them, using both reason and the Scriptures. Even so, even among orthodox Christians, the fine details of this often mysterious and impenetrable doctrine admit of some noteworthy variations, including about the process or mechanism by which Adam's corruption is disseminated and what role baptism plays in regard to original sin. Vermigli wades into these issues with great reverence, surveying many divergent opinions among the Fathers (Augustine, especially) and Schoolmen, and sometimes borrowing a point or offering options as a possible counter to a favored one. His basic Protestant presuppositions naturally color his opinion as to what he finds most sensible among any set of arguments.

Augustine considered the Pelagians a significant threat to the established doctrines of the Church. He wrote numerous treatises against representatives of this sect, mainly between the years 412 and 429, attacking their positions on free will and original sin.[4] In these he touched on the creation of the soul, what is and is not natural for a human being, grace and the remission of sins, problems posed by

---

4. Conveniently, most of Augustine's extensive writings against the Pelagians have been gathered together into one volume and translated in *Saint Augustine: Anti-Pelagian Writings*, trans. Peter Holmes, Robert Wallis, and Benjamin Warfield, 1ˢᵗ ser., vol. 5 of *Nicene and Post-Nicene Fathers*, ed. Philip Schaff (Grand Rapids, MI: Eerdmans, 1980 repr.) (hereafter cited as NPNF).

original sin to marriage, and the concept of concupiscence. Throughout these works he builds up a composite
depiction of Pelagianism and a delineation of his own the-
ories. In regard to the latter, he is not always as precise or
consistent as he should be, as Vermigli himself observes.
However, in a treatise titled *On Heresies*, written in 428 at
the prompting of a certain deacon named Quodvultdeus,
who desired an account of all known heresies, Augustine
provides a useful overview of Pelagian heresies as he grew
to understand them, including brief mention of those
having to do with original sin. Among Protestants of the
Reformed persuasion, as Vermigli was, this work found a
champion and commentator in scholar-theologian Lambert Daneau (1530–95).[5] Best known for his writings on
witchcraft, physics, and ethics, Daneau also was drawn to
Augustine's exposition of heresies as a way of advocating
for ecclesiastical discipline in his own day. He expands Augustine's section on the Pelagians, and in the process con-

---

5. Lambert Daneau, *D. Aurelii Augustini Hiponensis Episcopi liber
De haeresibus, ad Quodvultdeum…emendatus et commentariis illustratus, a quo eodem additae sunt haereses ab orbe condito ad constitutum
Papismum et Mahumetismum, etiam ea quae hic erant ab Augustino
praetermissae* (Geneva: Eustache Vignon, 1578), 215ᵛ–217ʳ. For bi-
ographical information on Daneau, one can consult the following:
Paul de Félice, *Lambert Daneau (de Baugency-sur-Loire), Pasteur et
Professeur en Théologie 1530–1595: Sa Vie, Ses Ouvrages, Ses Lettres In-
édites* (Paris: G. Fischbacher, 1881); and Olivier Fatio, "Lambert Daneau," in *Shapers of Religious Traditions in Germany, Switzerland, and
Poland, 1560–1600*, ed. Jill Raitt (New Haven, CT: Yale University
Press, 1981), 105–19. See also Olivier Fatio, *Nihil Pulchrius Ordine:
contribution à l'étude de l'établissement de la discipline ecclésiastique aux
Pay-Bas, ou Lambert Daneau aux Pays-Bas (1581–1583)* (Leiden: Brill,
1971); and Olivier Fatio, *Méthode et théologie. Lambert Daneau. Les
débuts de la scolastique réformée* (Genève: Droz, 1976).

structs a well-ordered list and succinct summation of the Pelagians' doctrines concerning original sin, at least those he found most dangerous and contrary to the Reformed faith. For our purposes, therefore, Daneau's "Reformed" expansion on Augustine's summation offers welcome signposts to lead us through Vermigli's work.

In his commentary, Daneau explains that the Pelagians hastened their descent into heresy when they began to establish *hypotheses* or axioms not dependent on the Scriptures but arising from their own preferences and definitions. According to Daneau, the Pelagians include one axiom, primary to all the others, which is fundamental to all the errors that follow: they hold that Adam would have died even if he had not sinned, because it was inherent to his condition to do so. In other words, death for Adam and all humankind is natural. We may not immediately grasp the significance of this axiom as the wellspring from which can flow a torrent of heretical dogmas, but Daneau considers it a ploy meant to support certain erroneous Pelagian positions, namely, that sin does not merit the penalty of death, and that Adam did not pass on death or sin to his posterity. Daneau counters these ideas by pointing to Romans 5:12, where Paul proclaims, "as by one man sin entered into the world, and death by sin, and so death went over all men; in whom all men have sinned."[6] Daneau likewise believes that Romans 5:12 con-

---

6. This is the translation from Thomson's Geneva Bible, following Theodore Beza's Latin. On the possibility that the Greek text means *because of Adam all sinned* instead of *in Adam all sinned*, see Vorster, "Calvin's Modification," 50. But Beza argues vehemently against this interpretation in his annotations, citing parallels to the grammar and quoting Augustine. He also points out that, if *because* is meant, v. 15

tradicts the Pelagian view that the sin of Adam harmed no one but himself, except to the extent that his posterity may be prone to imitate him. In the Pelagian point of view, Christ's contribution consisted merely in providing a counter-example to Adam and teaching us to live well, thereby "matching the medicine and pain-remedy to the type of wound." This, Daneau says, allows these heretics to deny the existence of original sin or its transmission from parents to children through procreation. The Pelagians furthermore teach that lust or concupiscence (Augustine's word to define original sin) is natural to us, and that it is good and not something for which we should feel shame. They say this to undermine the view held by some (not Vermigli, however,) that original sin is derived from the desire of the parents experienced during the conjugal act. The Pelagians point out that God himself ordained marriage as an institution and made it holy. Daneau, however, turns to David's lament at Psalm 51:7 ("I was born in iniquity, and in sin hath my mother conceived me") to support his view that after the Fall of Adam even the spousal desire in the marriage act is tainted before God, seeing that man and woman cannot help but sin.

The Pelagians also teach that infants do not in any way inherit original sin from their parents, contrary, Daneau says, to the aforementioned Romans 5:12. He also cites Ephesians 2:2 in this regard, where Paul states that all are born children of wrath by nature. It is also the Pelagian position that the unbaptized infants of the faithful

---

does not create a mirror contrast, since there Paul is not asserting that Christ saves his people from death by offering a model to imitate, but through the power of his death as a free gift.

will be saved and enjoy eternal life of some blessed quality, though this outside the kingdom of Heaven. Daneau finds two foolish errors in this doctrine: first, the idea that the children of the faithful will invariably attain salvation, and second, this unsupported notion of a secondary state and locale of eternal existence. The Church Fathers understandably hastened to the defense of the dignity of the sacrament of baptism, he adds, but in doing so they themselves rushed headlong into another error, "meeting with Scylla while trying to avoid Charybdis." They insisted that all unbaptized infants who die meet with eternal damnation, which led them in turn to posit the absolute necessity of baptism for salvation and the "power of the work worked" for the remission of sins, transferring to the earthly element of water what only the grace of God can confer.

In dealing with Pelagian error, Daneau does not mention Albert Pighius, but Vermigli addresses the Pelagian and extra-Pelagian doctrines put forward by him as a way to add immediate relevancy to his argument. Pighius published a work in 1541 titled *Controversiae* in which he set forth many unusual opinions, some original, some derivative, about central Christian doctrines. The first controversy of the sixteen treats the problem of original sin, termed variously in Latin as *peccatum originis* and *peccatum originale*, depending on the perspective.[7] Both Protestant and Catholic theologians alike balked at his conclusions and

---

7. Albert Pighius, "De peccato originis controversia," in *Controversiarum praecipuarum in comitiis Ratisponensibus tractatarum et quibus nunc potissimum exagitatur Christi fides et religio, diligens, et luculenta explicatio* (Cologne: Melchior Novesianus, 1542), fols. i^r–xxix^r.

disparagingly labeled him semi-Pelagian.[8] Not only did he receive an extensive rebuff from Calvin (parts of the *Controversiae* were directed at the 1539 *Institutes*), the Council of Trent likewise mentions him as an adherent to heretical teachings about sin. His *Controversiae* appeared on Catholic lists of banned books.[9] His work, therefore, in part occasioned Vermigli's essay.

Vermigli begins his discussion by laying out the positions of his opponents, whom he identifies as Pelagians and Anabaptists (he never again mentions the latter in the *Loci* selections, though their ideas on adult baptism are taken into account) (section 1). According to Vermigli, the Pelagians deny that there is any such thing as original sin for the following reasons: 1) Adam paid for his sin himself; 2) children do not pay for the sins of their parents; 3) God would not create a body in sin; 4) God himself instituted marriage, so it cannot be the medium through which sin is spread; and 5) the Scriptures call the children of the faithful *holy*. The Pelagians say that sin is a willful transgression against God's Law, that is to say, it must involve an intentional act against what is written in Scripture. As such, sin cannot be something passed on through body as if a physical object or part of the seed; it represents something actually committed by a human being compelled by inner motivations of rebellion. Thus, all

---

8. On the complex history of this designation and its use against Pighius, see Irena Backus and Aza Goudriaan, "*Semipelagianism*: The Origins of the Term and Its Passage into the History of Heresy," *Journal of Ecclesiastical History* 65, no. 1 (2014): 25–46.

9. Anthony Lane, "Albert Pighius's Controversial Work on Original Sin," *Reformation and Renaissance Review* 4, no. 1 (2002): 29–61.

individuals commit their own sins in conscious violation of the Law (something infants cannot do). If Adam plays a role in the matter, it is that he provides a model of transgression that his posterity imitates.

The Pelagians still must explain how death entered the world. They do so, Vermigli says, by assigning it to the natural state of Adam and Eve. Humans die because it is in their nature to do so, they say, not because Adam introduced death through his fall (section 2). Adam's first sin and the presence of death among human beings remain unconnected. Furthermore, the Pelagians hold that human nature is not sinful from birth, since, for sin to really exist, it must be actualized in the form of intentional rebellion against God's Law; infants, who lack a formed intellect or will, cannot sin. Simply to have the potential or the disposition for sin, a corrupt nature, in their view, does not constitute sin. They especially object to calling something *sin* that we could not avoid. It is abominable to think that an infant could sin unwittingly. Pelagians also question what makes Adam's one sin alone transferrable or significant, but not every sin of every ancestor (sections 3–5).

This misunderstanding of human nature is for Vermigli the crux of the problem with the Pelagian view, and the source from which all their other false notions flow (as Daneau also says). If the wages of sin is *death*, as the Scriptures teach, and if Christ, the new Adam, effects the *regeneration* of his people through his death and resurrection, then Genesis tells how mankind arrived at its dilemma by drawing the connection between sin and death. Vermigli regards Adam as he was originally created a whole person, supported by the gracious and supportive gifts of God to fulfill his ordained purpose, but not subject to death. God kept him in this condition. Adam's sin deprived him of these supports, as God withdrew them, and exposed him and human nature on the whole to self-reliance, weakness, lack of spirituality, decay, and death. Human beings thus became incapable of carrying out their supervisory role in the world and now stand at odds with creation. This is the corrupt state into which all are born, and for which they need to be reborn in Christ. The fact that infants sometimes die, Vermigli notes, further evinces that they have sin, as do scriptural connections between baptism and circumcision, both seals of renewal extended to infants (section 4).

The Pelagians do recognize that Adam has impacted his posterity negatively, but only in the sense that we are drawn to imitate his sin. Pighius diverges from the Pelagians on this point, choosing to define original sin as a guilt or legal liability derived from Adam's transgression, but not an actual sin of the one being born (section 5). Thus, he envisions two kinds of sin that alter our standing before God: one that Adam committed and which is placed on our account (as if we are paying the price for someone else's sin), and another of the sort that we commit when we are old enough to know rules and willfully violate them. Infants only have the first. What the orthodox view sees as fallen mankind's innate, inherent enmity against God, those affections and desires that control our bodies, minds, and souls, Pighius considers the "basic building-blocks of our nature" (section 6). They do not reflect a corrupt nature. Thus, those dying in infancy are only obligated by Adam's sin, according to Pighius, and so in the afterlife continue in an intermediate blessed state, free from the torments of Hell though still not existing directly in the presence of God.

Vermigli objects to this idea of transferred guilt, noting that the Scriptures everywhere make it clear that all of Adam's posterity is born into sin. They do not have to commit a sin to be sinful, they already have sin within them. Although originally in the Garden God did not create human beings with a corrupt, lustful, self-assertive nature, now all are born enslaved to such a nature, and "the imagination of their hearts from infancy is evil" (section 7). This exposes the fallacy of Pighius's analogy of the prince who freed his slave and gave him riches in exchange for loyalty (section 5). This assumes that the original parents were held in bondage (section 8). Instead, Vermigli prefers the analogy of a wolf, which, even as a pup, when it has done none of its potential damage, still has within it the seeds of evil and thus must be destroyed. Therefore, when Vermigli defines sin as "anything that opposes the Law of God," he is refuting the notion that sin is something that must be actualized by the will to qualify as a sin; it is, instead, a "propensity, inclination, natural bent, and proclivity to the doing of evil." Augustine calls it *concupiscence*. It is the rapacity lurking already in the wolf pup. It is the venom of the snake not yet used (sections 8–9).

Here, to make sense of the argument, we have to understand the commonly held anthropological view of the time. For Vermigli and Augustine alike, a human being is composed of body, the lower or "crasser" parts of the soul where the affections reside (this is the animating, sensing part of a person), and the higher part of the soul, the mind, where reason and the will reside. All of these were damaged in Adam's sin and all in concert resist the standard set by God from the beginning for human existence. Human beings have a natural bent that is "prone to all depravity" (sections 10–11). This *damage* can be explained as the just punishment for Adam's rebellion, when God removed the divine gifts and grace that he gave to the first parents as an endowment so that they could fulfill his wishes. Corruption, formerly alien to the human condition because of these gifts, came rushing in once those gifts were removed. Adam and Eve then passed on this new image, stripped from its original divinely bestowed gifts, to their posterity. Thus, instead of culpability they passed on a weak nature with a propensity to assert itself over the demands of God (sections 10–15).

Vermigli stresses that human beings were not corrupt as they were originally created. While Pighius and the Pelagians consider self-assertion and willfulness to be an inherent part of human nature, to Vermigli these reflect an unnatural corruption, a concupiscence (as Augustine says) not in accord with the image of God. The Father endowed the first parents with his image "so that he can adorn us with divine properties, that is to say, with righteousness, wisdom, goodness, and patience" (section 13). These gifts graciously given equipped mankind in its intelligence, memory, and will to govern creation well. Once Adam fell and lost these gifts, all infants come into the world with appetites raging out of control and resistant to God's Word. They are ignorant of their place in the world, unwilling to be subject to God, incapable of governing the baser impulses through reason, corrupt in both the fleshly and spiritual aspects of the mind. Scripture affirms this in infants when it says in numerous passages that all are born into sin. Although this sin is not an action per se, it is nevertheless an unrighteous and concupiscent disposition. It is the role of baptism to break its power and nullify the imputation of it in the process of regeneration. Baptism "seals in its recipients the remission of guilt and offense, grace, the Spirit, the ingrafting into Christ, and the right to eternal life" (section 46). Even so, the baptized find that the struggle against sin is a lifelong process to "put on the new man." The person assuming the new man, in other words, begins to recover the lost virtues, those original supports, by becoming more and more conformed to the image of Christ (sections 14–19).

Vermigli bolsters his case against Pighius by appealing to the Church Fathers, who are nearly unanimous in denying our innocence at birth (section 21). They base their teaching on such passages as Psalm 51:7, where David laments being born in iniquity, or Job's rhetorical question, "Who is able to make clean that which is conceived of an unclean seed?" (Job 14:4). The Pelagians erroneously evoked Basil of Caesarea (329/30–79) as a partisan of theirs because of some statements that he made about evil's origins in the will.[10] But Basil, says Vermigli, only intends to refute the Manichaeans' treatment of evil as something substantial, not to suggest that infants are exempted from the contamination of original sin because they cannot yet

---

10. For this, see section 22. Basil raises this point in what has traditionally been labeled Homily 9, with the title *Homilia quod Deus non est auctor malorum* (*That God Is Not the Author of Sin*), but which has since been renumbered as 336 by Paul Fedwick in his *Basil of Caesarea: Christian, Humanist, Ascetic* (Toronto: Pontifical Institute of Mediaeval Studies, 1981), 3–20. A translation is available in Nonna Verna Harrison, *St. Basil the Great: On the Human Condition* (Crestwood, NY: St. Vladimir's Seminary Press, 2005), 65–80.

exercise their will.[11] Basil is clear throughout his writings that evil was not natural to humans as originally created, but an "accident" (an Aristotelian term) to their nature, and that infants need to be cleansed of this contamination through baptism (sections 22–23).

In Vermigli's opinion, Pighius in many ways surpasses the Pelagians in heresy. He certainly departs from his Roman Catholic brethren, whose traditions surrounding infant burial and baptism assume a belief in original sin (section 23). Pelagius also teaches that human beings as originally created were whole *without* the divine gifts afterwards bestowed by the Father. When Adam sinned, Pighius argues, the extra gifts were removed and human beings reverted from a supernatural state to their original wholeness (section 24). Thus, as each individual enters the world, he arrives whole and as God intended them to be. They do not sin until their will and reason are so formed that they can intentionally violate God's Law. If an infant dies, there is no reason he or she should be punished.

The removal of the divine gifts that lead to the damage of human nature grounds Vermigli's entire argument about original sin. In section 25 he qualifies what he means by *removal* in a succinct expression of the Reformed doctrine of natural knowledge.[12] The objection could be raised

---

11. The Manichaeans were a sect founded in the third century by Mani. They taught a radical dualism, an eternal conflict between a good Father of Lights and an evil Prince of Darkness. For an account, see especially Geo Widengren, *Mani and Manichaeism* (New York: Holt, Rinehart, and Winston, 1965).

12. For Calvin's treatment of the noetic effects of sin and residual knowledge after the Fall, see *Inst.* (1559) 2.2.12–24.

that a scheme that includes the deprivation of the divine gifts necessary to make human beings whole would so ruin the human race that it could not function or build a civilized society. Vermigli rejects this conclusion. God has left a residual amount of his gifts in human beings so that they can search for and, in a limited way, discover what is good and just. Many pagan philosophers and statesmen espoused ethical behavior and created commendable laws because a glimmer of God's grace remained in them, restraining them, nudging them to the truth.

In all of this, Vermigli has been endeavoring to establish two categories of sin (following Augustine): we commit *actual* sins when we have the capacity to willfully violate the commands of God, but we are also born with a concupiscence or evil disposition, which is itself sin. The latter exists in us because God withdrew those gifts and grace that made us able to fulfill our purpose in the world as he intended. After establishing the existence and nature of this sin, Vermigli spends much of the rest of the work on how this sin spreads from person to person (sections 26–32). He notes differing opinions, including the idea that the act of procreation itself spreads sin because it involves lust and thus is inherently evil. But Vermigli disagrees that legitimate marital sex necessarily contains sin (recall that Daneau favored this opinion) and prefers to look elsewhere for an explanation. He is attracted to the conjecture that since corruption resides primarily in the flesh, it is through seed that sin spreads. The Scriptures seem to support this claim in numerous places. The flesh, then, which both contains and spreads its corruption through seed, in turn contaminates the soul whenever it comes into contact with it. The magnificence of Christ's work lies in the restoration of both soul and body through the various "seeds" that he offers: baptism, for one, but primarily the Word. Both of these instruments of grace initiate the process of regeneration in God's people, so that the guilt of original sin is no longer imputed to eternal death. The remnants of corruption persist in the regenerate, however, and the corrupt self is never fully defeated until we experience our resurrection.

In this section Vermigli also considers the arguments of the Pelagians against the existence of original sin. The Pelagians reject the idea that God would continue to punish the sin of Adam in his progeny, since it would be unjust for him to pass judgment twice for one and the same sin. In support of this, they point to Nahum 1:9 (section 33). Vermigli agrees that God would not do this but reiterates a subtle point that is easily missed: all individuals are born in sin because their natures, deprived of God's gracious support after the Fall, stand opposed to God's Word and Law. This disposition of the mind, soul, and flesh alone *is* a sin deserving punishment. It is a pervasive attitude and stance of rebellion. In a sense, everyone has contracted this sin from Adam as one might contract the plague from a sick person: the sickness is one's own, but it has its source in the original person suffering from the plague. This doctrinal schematic resolves the apparent contradiction to the doctrine of original sin posed by Ezekiel 18:20, where it is written that "the son will not bear the iniquity of the father" (sections 34 and 41). Yes, Vermigli says, people bear their own sins, not those of Adam. They only inherited sinful natures from Adam. Descendants are not receiving punishment for something their ancestors did, but for the sinfulness inherent to their nature from birth. God is not punishing the innocent for the sins of another, since everyone has their own sin. Conversely, when it is stated in the Law that God punishes sins to the third and fourth generation, we should understand this to represent a truism that sins have enduring effects on a family or people, either through the assumption of certain ancestral traits or because of the long-lasting ramifications resulting from a sin. But this merely serves as a call to repentance, since the children themselves must hate God for him to punish them. It is the case, however, that often they do hate him.

Those who object to the doctrine of original sin also ask how sin passes through the holy (sections 38–39). Are not the faith of the parents and the divinely established institution of marriage sufficient to hinder the transmission of original sin? Vermigli agrees that the children of godly parents have a more stable home in which to be nurtured in the faith, and that they benefit from the covenant originally made to Adam. Still (and again), even in the children of godly parents the cooperation of body and soul has broken down because the soul is "no longer strengthened with its original endowments." The Fall, as Vermigli has reiterated throughout, meant the loss of the power and gifts to live in accord with God's will. In the end, however, only God knows which children belong to him and which do not; while human beings see only the visible Church, God alone knows the invisible Church.

Vermigli looks also to the problem of the accrual of guilt: the Pelagians hold that, if sin is passed from generation to generation, those who live later must be at a severe disadvantage in comparison to Adam's earlier descendants, since they have accumulated more sin and its implications from more ancestors (section 43). Vermigli shows that the

Church has traditionally denied an aggregate of sins in Adam's posterity, or even that the sins of one's immediate or "proximate" parents pass to their children. Augustine taught that children draw original sin from their parents in the form of a corrupt nature; it is this sin, this failure to conform to what God intended them to be, for which God holds newborns accountable. Whether the parents' other sins influence their children in any way is totally determined by God, seeing that every goodness in us depends on God's grace and helps. Once again, this distinction in our parents' sins grounds Vermigli's main argument. In his view, the Pelagians (and Pighius after them) have an inadequate definition of sin, given that they do not recognize that the base inclination with which every human being comes into the world is sinfulness per se and subject to God's judgment. This basic depravity of nature is the root sin from which all actual sins derive.

Vermigli's treatment of original sin concludes with a discursive piece that he included with his commentary on Romans 5:12, already cited above (sections 44–58). In reference to this verse, Vermigli addresses three questions: 1) what is sin; 2) who is responsible for sin entering the world; and 3) how is sin spread. For the first question, Vermigli covers ground familiar from the main section of this *locus*, with reference made to mankind's original state, the image of God within, and the difference between original contagion and actual sins. The second question is handled by underscoring Paul's antithesis between Adam and Jesus, the one who introduced sin and damaged human nature, and the one who restores human nature (section 45). As for how sin is propagated and spread from soul to soul, Vermigli records four opinions on the matter (section 47).

Here it is interesting to note the problems posed in explaining the propagation of original sin by Jesus's birth to Mary. If the soul passes corrupt from the parents, then would Jesus have inherited Mary's depravity (section 48)? Or if God creates the soul damaged and corrupted, why did he spare Jesus? And what would this say about God? The option that most makes sense to Vermigli is the idea that God creates the soul sinless but the soul contracts sin from the body immediately upon being joined with it because the soul lacks spiritual supports (section 49). Furthermore, death affects the soul when God strips his grace from it and deprives it of the life as he intended (sections 50–51). Death, therefore, is not natural for human beings because God would have continued to support Adam with the grace of immortality.[13] This fits well with Vermigli's main thesis regarding original sin.

Vermigli concludes with a fascinating discussion of creatures and the Fall (sections 52–58). Almost all agree that the human race fell in Adam. In what sense, he asks, did creation itself fall? Creation does not possess a higher soul or aspire to the image of God. Yet, according to Paul, it grieves and is vexed because of us and waits our final revelation as children of God. Meanwhile, it experiences decay and extremes, poison and disease. The angels themselves, whom we should imagine are in a blessed state, seem anxious for our restoration. Vermigli accepts that the

---

13. Calvin, *Inst.* (1536), 20–21, explains it this way: "Adam, parent of us all, was created in the image and likeness of God [Gen. 1:26–27]. That is, he was endowed with wisdom, righteousness, holiness, and was so clinging by these gifts of grace to God that he could have lived forever in Him, if he had stood fast in the uprightness God had given him."

angels live in happiness, yet they also feel frustrated at the seeming unending nature of their work, their involvement and dealings with corruption and mortality. They are blissful by nature, but in regard to their tasks they are "subject to vanity," that is, they cannot finish them. Mankind mismanages and ruins creation and has thrown the world into chaos. Everything is out of sorts. Figuratively speaking, therefore, nature, which wants to serve godly masters, instead suffers under its evil overlords. Nature helped the Israelites as they fled from Egypt. It responded with joy to the birth of Christ, with turmoil at his death; when the Savior arose from the tomb, the earth quaked and the angels appeared; a cloud facilitated his ascension. The Scriptures foretell that at his return all creation will be renewed and the sun will shine seven times greater. The long dark night brought about by Adam's sin will finally be dispelled, the injury done to creation undone, and the glory of God's image will return once again to the human race.[14]

ABOUT THE TRANSLATION AND SOURCES

For the Latin text, I relied on the first edition published in London in 1576 at the press of John Kyngston under the title *Loci communes, ex variis ipsius acuthoris et libris in unum volumen collecti, et quatuor classes distributi.* For difficult passages, I consulted the only vernacular edition, translated by Anthony Marten and published in London

---

14. Cf. Calvin, *Inst.* (1559), 1.15.4, where he builds the case that Christ effects the renewal of knowledge, righteousness, and holiness, the summation of the light of God's image in us, from his reading of Col. 3:10 and Eph. 4:24. See also his commentary on Gen. 1:26.

in 1583 at the press of H. Denham and H. Middleton under the title *The Common Places . . . divided into foure principall parts: with a large addition of manie theologicall and necessarie discourses, some never extant before.* The latter corrects some of the original's errors of section numbering and division, and I have followed its modifications when appropriate. In a few places, I checked the text against the 1622 Heidelberg edition published by Daniel and David Aubry and Clement Schleich.[15] The goal throughout has been to create a translation that flows with an English style familiar to the modern reader while maintaining the integrity of the theological language as much as possible. It is a delicate balancing act that may offend some who are steeped in the writings of Reformed orthodoxy, but it will hopefully make Peter Martyr Vermigli available to a wider audience. I am grateful to Dr. Atria Larson of Greystone Theological Institute for graciously reading over the translation and checking for errors and omissions, and for pointing out instances in which the Latin depends more on medieval nuances of meaning than classical or patristic. One such example is the word *noxa*, which the reader will find translated here as *a liability* (e.g., the beginning of section 5), based on medieval legal terminology. In other instances, I have allowed Vermigli's source (often Augustine) or the immediate context to dictate how a word should be translated.

---

15. A detailed description of the fourteen editions of the *Loci* can be found in John Patrick Donnelly, SJ, Robert Kingdon, and Marvin Anderson, *A Bibliography of the Works of Peter Martyr Vermigli* (Ann Arbor, MI: Edwards Brothers, 1990), 98–126.

The sections covering original sin in the *Loci* are adapted from Vermigli's commentaries on Genesis, Romans, and 1 Corinthians, the first editions of which are as follows:

1. *In primum librum Mosis, qui vulgo Genesis dicitur commentarii doctissimi.* Zurich: [C. Froschauer], 1569;

2. Vermigli, Peter Martyr. *In Epistolam S. Pauli Apostoli ad Romanos[...]commentarii doctissimi.* Zurich: [A. Gesner], 1559;

3. *In selectissimam D. Pauli priorem ad Corinthios Epistolam[...]commentarii doctissimi.* Zurich: [C. Froschauer], 1551.

In these editions, chapters 1–43 of this translation (1–44 of the Latin edition) derive from Vermigli's digression on original sin at Genesis 8 (36ʳ–38ᵛ) and his comments on the phrase "as through one man's trespass" at Romans 5:17 (274–316). Chapters 44–49 (45–50 of the Latin edition) are taken from Vermigli's comments on Rom. 5:12 and the words "As through one man . . ." (251–58). Chapter 50 (51) interrupts the flow by drawing from Vermigli's comments on 1 Cor. 15:21 and the phrase "as death came through a man" (408ᵛ–409ᵛ), while 51 (52) returns to Romans 5:12 and the phrase "and death through sin" (258–59). Chapters 52–58 (Chapters 53–59 of the Latin edition) derive from Vermigli's commentary on Romans 8:20, where he interprets the phrase "all things are subject to vanity through sin" (501–08).

In order to better organize the material for the modern reader, eighteen new "chapter" divisions have been created (the entire text is a "chapter" in the original *Loci Communes*). I have devised the chapter names myself; in order to make it clear that they are not original to Vermigli, they are all enclosed in brackets.

PETER MARTYR VERMIGLI: SECOND PART OF THE COMMON PLACES

FIRST CHAPTER

On sin, especially original sin, and
the general corruption of human nature

[CHAPTER 1:
THE PELAGIANS ON
HUMAN NATURE]

1. To begin with, we will ask the question whether or not original sin is a real thing, since some utterly deny that it even exists. After that, we will say what it is. Lastly, we will examine what properties it has, how it is passed on as an inheritance to posterity, and how it is forgiven or remitted.

As to the first matter, we must remember that, both in the Scriptures and in the Fathers, it has various names. In Romans 7 [vv. 8, 23], it is called *sin*, and *the law of the members*, and *concupiscence*. Elsewhere, it is termed *the lack of original righteousness, the corruption of nature, an evil imagination* [Gen. 8:21], *the kindling* [of hate and evil, Gen. 37:8], *a weakness of nature, the law of the flesh*, and others of such a kind. Long ago, the Pelagians used to deny the existence of this sin; today the Anabaptists do the same. Their arguments run roughly as follows: first, they say, the Fall of Adam received its sufficient punishment, and there is no reason why God would want to exact a penalty for it from his posterity, especially since in the prophet Nahum it is written that "God does not punish the same sin twice, for it is enough that he punished it once" [Nah. 1:9]. Second, they argue that the Scriptures say that the son will not bear the iniquity of the father, but the same soul that sins will likewise die [Ez. 18:20]. Next, they argue that the body, when it is formed in the womb, is the workmanship of God, and there is no reason that it should be blamed. To the contrary, they say, we should admire it to the utmost, along with marveling that it has a soul created or infused by God. They also assert that we should not consider the means of its propagation as a bad thing, since marriage is commended by Scriptures, and from the beginning God bid mankind to procreate.

In view of this, they ask through what cracks, among so many defenses of innocence, sin could insinuate itself. They add also that Paul in I Corinthians [7:14], when he was urging a believing wife to remain with an unbelieving husband should the spouse be willing, says among other things, "Your children are holy." They object that they cannot be holy if they are born in sin. Therefore, those who are born from believing parents cannot inherit original sin from them. Additionally, they maintain that in common parlance a sin is something that is said, done, or desired contrary to the Law of God, and that it is not a sin unless it is voluntary. Accordingly, John says in his epistle [1 John 3:4], "sin is iniquity," to which is contrasted equity or fairness, which cannot be reckoned as anything than that which is contained in the Law. Thus, sin is the transgression of the Law. None of these things, they argue, properly fits with infants who are just being born.[1]

---

1. For this argument, see Pighius, "De peccato originis controversia," fols. iv[r] and vii[r-v] (to refute Anselm's view that sin is a lack of original righteousness).

Nor do they agree with what some people say, that this sin is transferred through the flesh or body. According to them, flesh and body are by nature senseless things and not a suitable receptacle for sin.[2] And to bolster their fabrication, they add that we should assign those things which Paul says in Romans 5 [v. 12] to those sins which are called *actual*.[3] Furthermore, in reference to Paul's statement about sin entering the world through one man, they claim this is because posterity imitated him and followed his example.

2. Guided by these and similar arguments, they deny that there is any such thing as original sin. The death and afflictions of this life, which are usually thought of as indications confirming original sin, they say are the result of natural causes, such as is the temperature of the elements and humoral fluids.[4] Therefore, they claim that for us to

---

2. See especially Pighius, "De peccato originis controversia," fols. xvii[r-v].

3. He is distinguishing *actual* sins, that is, sins that a person actually and actively commits, from the persistent, innate stain or corruption of *original* sin. The latter gives birth to the former, as a tree produces fruit. The reformers followed Augustine in this distinction (e.g., *De peccatorum meritis et remissione* 1.11 [*On the Merits*, NPNF, 5:19]) and in calling this corruption *concupiscence* or *cupidity*, as Vermigli here, seeing the paradigmatic relationship between original and actual sins expressed succinctly at James 1:15.

4. It was a longstanding belief, derived from ancient Greek physicians and philosophers, that the elements (earth, water, wind, and fire), recognizable from their so-called *temperatures* of dry, wet, cold, and hot, are mirrored in the elements and their humoral agents within the human body. The balance of these humors in turn produce temperaments. Vermigli has in mind the arguments of Pighius that, essentially, proneness to evil is not evil, at "De peccato originis controversia,"

relate those things to the Fall of Adam is a mere contrivance. They also consider it most absurd to posit some sin that cannot in any way be avoided. Lastly, they say, if by that rationale we are said to have sinned in Adam, because we were in his loins, as Hebrews [7:5] states that Levi paid tithes in the loins of Abraham, by one and the same rationale we may say that we were in the loins of other forefathers, from whom we descended by procreation. So, there is no reason why the sin of Adam should be distributed to us more than that of our grandfather, great-grandfather, great-great-grandfather, or any of our progenitors. By this logic, they argue, the condition of those who are born in the last times could be viewed as most unhappy, since they have borne the iniquities of all their elders. To their mind, this debunks the notion of original sin.

We disagree, however, and will prove that original sin exists from many scriptural testimonies. In Genesis 6, God says this: "My spirit will not quarrel with man, because he is flesh" [vv. 3, 5]. And again: "The imagination of the thoughts of their heart is only evil all day long." And in the eighth chapter [v. 21]: "The imagination of their heart is evil from childhood." These words indicate that in our nature when we are born there clings some vice. David also says, "Behold I am conceived in iniquities, and in sins my mother conceived me" [Ps. 51:7]. Nothing can be clearer than this testimony. Jeremiah says in the seventeenth chapter, "The heart of man is depraved and perverse and broken" [v. 3]. And Jeremiah as well as Job curse the day in which they were born in the world, because they perceived that the origin and fount of vices sprang up

fol. xvi^v.

4

along with them [Job 3:3; Jer. 20:14]. Job, moreover, gives an absolutely clear testimony of our inborn uncleanness when he says, "Who is able to make clean that which is conceived of an unclean seed?" [Job 14:4]. And our Savior says, "Unless someone is born of water and the Holy Spirit, that person will not enter into the kingdom of Heaven" [John 3:3]. As a potter does not refashion any vase unless he sees that the existing one was fashioned poorly, so Christ would not wish us to be generated anew, unless he saw that we were begotten in an unhappy state.

[CHAPTER 2: ADAM'S WHOLENESS BEFORE THE FALL]

3. He bears witness to this in another passage, saying, "What is born from flesh is flesh; and what is born of spirit is spirit" [John 3:6]. By these words he wanted us to understand that we need the rebirth of the spirit because formerly we had only a birth of the flesh. Paul, in the sixth chapter to the Romans [v. 2], says, "Therefore, we should not remain in sin, because we are now dead to it." He proves it from baptism: "For, whoever of us," he says, "is baptized in Christ Jesus, are baptized into his death, to the end that we might die to sin, and so that our old man might be crucified and the body of sin might be abolished" [Rom. 6:3]. And when children are baptized, even from this do we have testimony that there is sin in them; otherwise, Paul's explanation for how baptism works makes no sense. He follows the same line of reasoning in Colossians, where he says that we are "circumcised with a circumcision made without hands, through the removal of sins of the flesh from the body, being buried with Christ in

baptism" [Col. 2:12]. He compares baptism with circumcision and says that those who are baptized are cleansed of
sin from the body. There can be no doubt that those who
are baptized are baptized to the remission of sins. And circumcision, which in the old Law was done to children,
certainly was corresponding to our baptism. Concerning
circumcision, it is written, "The soul, whose flesh of the
foreskin is not circumcised on the eighth day, will surely die" [Gen. 17:14]. Wherefore, since children need the
sacrament that leads to regeneration and rebirth, we must
surmise that they are born under the power of sin.[1] Paul
says to the Ephesians that we are by nature the children of
wrath [Eph. 2:3]. Yet, God would only hate our nature if
it is contaminated by sin. And in the same passage, Paul,
with the gravest words, describes the horribleness of this
wrath: "We walk according to the prince of this world,
who has power in our hearts because of our stubbornness,
and therefore we do the will of the flesh of our mind"
[Eph. 2:2]. Augustine cites a passage also from 1 Corinthians [15:22], where it is said that Christ died for all.[2]
From this it follows that all were dead and have need of
his death. Moreover, it is wrong to exclude children from
the number for whom Christ died. But if you inquire of

---

1. See Augustine's arguments in this regard at *De gratia Christi, et de
peccato originali* 2.35 (*On the Grace of Christ and On Original Sin*,
NPNF, 5:250).

2. Augustine, *De diversis quaestionibus ad Simplicianum* 1.2.16 (*To
Simplician, on various questions*, 398), cites 1 Cor. 15:22 in support
of his argument that all posterity can trace the origin of their sin to
Adam. Though he alludes to the Corinthians passage, he likely has in
mind Rom. 5:12; on this see Keech, *The Anti-Pelagian Christology*, 80.

what sort they were for whom Christ died, the Apostle expressed it well enough in Romans, when he said they were weak, enemies of God, impious, sinners. We must include small children among this number if we want Christ to have died for them.

In addition, it seems that original sin is most clearly taught from Romans 7, where we find written the following: "The law is spiritual, but I am carnal, sold under sin" [v. 14]. Furthermore: "The good that I wish, I do not do; but the evil that I do not wish, this I do; yet it is not I who accomplish it, but the sin dwelling in me" [vv. 15, 17]. He also mentions the law of the members, which he complains drag him about as an unwilling captive [v. 23]. And in chapter 8 [v. 7] he says, "The disposition of the flesh is enmity against God; and it is not subject to the law of God, no, nor can it be." Even death, which small children suffer, sufficiently testifies that sin clings in them— unless we are willing to say that God punishes those who do not deserve it. Furthermore, a passage in Romans 5 contains a very clear testimony of original sin. Paul writes the following: "Through one man sin entered the world, and all without exception have sinned"; and "the wickedness of one person spread through all"; and "on account of the disobedience of one person many are considered sinners" [vv. 12–15]. Additionally, those who are grafted into Christ at the end of the same epistle are called wild olive trees [Rom. 11:17]. This metaphor indicates that man degenerated from the natural goodness that he had at the original creation. But if we have departed from our created nature, certainly we have inherited original sin. And above Paul accuses the whole race of mortals when he says, "There is none righteous, none understanding or seeking after God. All have fallen away and at the same time have become useless; there is not one who practices goodness, no, not one" [Rom. 3:10]. All these things sufficiently point to the utter corruption of human nature. From these testimonies of the Scriptures I think it is clear enough that there is original sin.

4. Next, I should dispose of the arguments of my adversaries. But first I think it will be of value to state clearly the definition of original sin. By carefully weighing and coming to grips with it, we will learn many things along the way that will help us dispel their arguments. First, we will rehearse the opinions of others; afterwards, we will reveal what seems right to us.

The Pelagians asserted that the sin of Adam did not flow down to posterity, except only by imitation. Augustine objected strongly to them and by many arguments showed that original sin is not merely the imitation of the sin of Adam.[3] If Paul had wanted to say that the first sin was spread in this manner, he would not have said that it flowed from Adam; rather, he would have said it came from the devil [Rom. 5:12]. It was the devil, after all, who first showed how to sin and gave form to it. Therefore, Christ in the Gospel of John says that the Jews, who were boasting themselves to be from father Abraham, are instead sons of the devil, because they do his works [John 8:41, 44]. From the beginning, the devil was a murderer;

---

3. Augustine, *De peccatorum meritis et remissione* 1.9 and 17 (*On the Merits*, NPNF, 5:18, 21); *De natura et gratia* 10 (On *Nature and Grace*, NPNF, 5:124); *De gratia Christi, et de peccato originali* 2.16 (*On the Grace of Christ and On Original Sin*, NPNF, 5:242); and *De nuptiis et concupiscentia* 2.45 (On *Marriage and Concupiscence*, NPNF, 5:301).

the Jews, in a similar vein, wished to kill Jesus although he did not deserve it. In this regard Augustine cites the passage from the second book of the Wisdom of Solomon [v. 24], that the envy of the devil brought death into the world, and his followers imitate him.[4]

Nevertheless, I do not give much credit to this latter saying, partly because the book is not in the canon, and partly because in the Greek text there is some ambiguity. There we do not find the word for *imitate*, but instead *experience* (πειράζουσι), that is, they experience that death. Even so, I agree with his argument that the first example of sin came from the devil. Furthermore, the Pelagian opinion is further refuted by the fact that Paul draws an antithesis between Christ and Adam [Rom. 5:18]. In that antithesis, the righteousness of Christ is not merely presented for us to imitate, but also that those who believe in him might be changed in mind, corrected in spirit, and emended in all their strength.[5] Because of this, in turn it is required, by analogy, that beyond his offering a bad example to posterity, Adam corrupted their nature, and (as Augustine says in his book *On the Merits and Forgiveness of Sins*) corrupted them with a certain consuming disease.[6] A third argument against the Pelagian view is this: even infants themselves die. For, as Paul says in Romans 6 [v. 23], "The payment of sin is death, but the gift of God is eternal

---

4. Augustine, *De nuptiis et concupiscentia* 2.45 (On *Marriage and Concupiscence*, NPNF, 5:301).

5. An allusion to Jesus's words recorded at Luke 10:27 and Mark 12:30.

6. For this section, Vermigli draws heavily from *De peccatorum meritis et remissione* 1.9–11 (*On the Merits*, NPNF, 5:18–19).

life through Christ Jesus our Lord." And in 1 Corinthians 15 [v. 56] he says, "The weapon of sin is death." Finally, baptism, which is given to small children, cannot be removing imitative sin from them; therefore, it is necessary that we posit in them another kind of sin, lest we think they are baptized in vain.

[CHAPTER 3:
PIGHIUS ON INFANT GUILT]

5. Another opinion was that which the teacher of the *Sentences* recounted in book two, the thirtieth distinction.[1] He talks about those who think that original sin is only a guilt or liability or obligation to which we are bound on account of the sin of Adam. These people do not acknowledge any actual fault or sin in those who are born, but only some liability and obligation, so that they die and are condemned because of Adam's sin.[2] Pighius almost seems to have revived this opinion. He denied that original sin is really a sin, since it is not a transgression of the Law, nor does it derive from the will.[3] Therefore, he posited that it

---

1. This is a reference to Peter Lombard's *Libri quattuor sententiarum* (*The Sentences*, 145–53), a theological handbook that was divided into chapters and numerous subsections called *distinctions*. The second book deals with creation.

2. See Augustine, *Contra Iulianum Pelagianum* 3.4.10 (*Against Julian the Pelagian*, 114–16). The point here can be summed up as follows: Some say that we are born answerable and liable for Adam's sin, but that we do not have our own actual sin until we commit a sin ourselves voluntarily.

3. As Vermigli observes in the next sentence, Pighius does in a sense admit that original sin is an actual sin, though he would say that it

is nothing but the sin of Adam, for which we his posterity become subject to damnation and death, and are made exiles from the kingdom of Heaven.[4] They also say death, the afflictions of this life, the desires of the heart, and other affections of this kind have their source in nature. So far is he from calling these sins that he proclaims them works of God, since God is the author of nature.[5] And he states that these things follow the humors and temperature of the body, and that which we see happening among brute beasts, happens also in the case of human beings so far as the flesh and duller powers of the mind are concerned.[6] They desire those things which tend toward their survival

---

was Adam who committed it, not the infant, since the infant with an unformed will cannot transgress the Law; see "De peccato originis controversia," fols. iv[r]–vii[v] and xv[v]. For Augustine on the distinction between original sin and actual sin, see *De peccatorum meritis et remissione* 1.11 (*On the Merits*, NPNF, 5:19).

4. Pighius's clearest assertion of this position appears at "De peccato originis controversia," fol. xxiv[r], where he is interpreting Rom. 5:12 in his own unique way. He asserts that we are all born under the judgment against Adam, that in him was that sin whereby we all sinned. All are born sinners, but not because of their *own* sin. See also the succinct expression of his view at fol. xxvi[r]: "Original sin is the sin of the originator of the human race, obviously Adam, whereby he made himself and us exiles from the kingdom of the heavenly Jerusalem, and rendered us subject to death and eternal damnation. And he embroiled us with him in all the calamities and miseries of human nature, from which the superabundance of the gifts of divine grace had rescued us and kept us immune. Because we are bound by the guilt of this one person, we are all born sinners. From this guilt, the grace of regeneration in Christ frees and absolves us."

5. Pighius, "De peccato originis controversia," fols. xii[v]–xv[r].

6. Pighius, "De peccato originis controversia," fol. xvii[r].

and which are pleasant and useful, whether they are in accord with reason or not; and they avoid those things that are the opposite to all that. Therefore, in Pighius's opinion, the only original fault lies with Adam's transgression, and he thinks that we are all born liable for this one transgression, yet not because of some vice, fault, or depravity that we have in ourselves.

He also asserts that those who die only obligated to the vice of Adam will not in any way be afflicted in the other life with physical punishment. He imagines (though he does not dare to affirm it consistently) that they experience a kind of natural happiness and blessedness, whether in this world or in some other reasonably pleasant place.[7] There, he says, they will live praising God and giving thanks, even though they are excluded from the kingdom of Heaven. He dreams that they will in no way complain about this disadvantage nor become sad because of it. He explains that this amounts to struggling against the will of God, which cannot happen without sin. And since, while they were living here, they had no corruption in their will, we cannot believe that they will have it in the other life. Moreover, that they will not suffer sensible punishment, he feels quite confident he has proven for two reasons: first, because they committed no evil act nor contaminated themselves with any corruption; second, because in this life no repentance or contrition is required for original sin.

And for this fiction he has this pretext, that we not take something as a sin unless we have a legitimate reason. In other words, it needs to be a thing spoken, done, or desired against the Law of God, and it must be voluntary,

---

7. Pighius, "De peccato originis controversia," fols. xxvii^r–xviii^r.

not something forced upon someone unwilling, but something that can be avoided. And since these things have no place in young children, there can be no sin in them. Nevertheless, he says that he does not deny the existence of original sin; to his mind it is the sin of Adam, and this is what brings condemnation and death on all of us. This is why I said that he seeks this as a pretext, because in reality I see that, though he says these things, he has other motivations. Since he attributes so much to free will, and has written so many things about the subject against us,[8] and since he sees that it is inconsistent if he openly admits to original sin (which all the godly teach), he conveniently hit upon this new idea.[9] But this is not altogether so new, seeing that the doctrine is discussed and rejected by the teacher of the *Sentences*.

Yet, to give more brilliant color to his invention, he draws a comparison to some generous prince, who not only frees one of his servants, but also endows him with a lordship, and enriches him with wealth that will extend to his posterity.[10] The prince only bids his servant to obey faithfully certain mandates. If he transgresses these, he should be aware that all those riches and benefits will be snatched from him, and he himself will be returned to servitude. This servant, being imprudent and ungrateful, violates the mandates of the prince. And so, not only is he

---

8. In 1542 Pighius published *De libero hominis arbitrio*. For the work and Calvin's reply, see John Calvin, *The Bondage and Liberation of the Will*.

9. Vermigli uses the word *sententia* (idea) here as a play on Lombard's *Sententiae*, that is, the *Sentences*.

10. Pighius, "De peccato originis controversia," fols. xiv^r–xxv^r.

made a servant as before, but also he begets children into servitude. But those children have no reason to complain about the servitude of the prince; rather, they have reason to give thanks because he treated their father so liberally. Concerning their father, however, they can feel the utmost grief, because he lost those endowments both for himself and for them. But that is not all. What if you add also that the liberality of the prince was so great that he invited the descendants of that ungrateful servant to the very same blessings, and even to far greater ones; and he invited them in such a way that he gladly sent his own son to summon them? This is our current situation, Pighius says. Adam was created by God so as to be capable of supernatural happiness. Nevertheless, when he held in contempt the commands of God, he was stripped of those supernatural gifts and was left to the first state of his own nature. And in that state also we were begotten, and thus on account of his sin we are condemned and die, exiled from the kingdom of Heaven, suffering many troubles, which are derived from the basic and essential principles of our nature. Therefore, we can complain about the first parent but not about God, since he was very generous toward him; but he was markedly generous when he called us again to himself, which is the utmost source of joy, through his one and only Son, and for our salvation willingly met death.

6. Yet, what I have said twice now, that infants die, especially counters this idea. Death has no rightful claim where there is no sin unless we want to say that God punishes the innocent. Paul confirms this assertion when he makes the case that sin was before the Law. "For, death," he says, "reigned from Adam unto Moses" [Rom. 5:14]. But in Pighius's opinion, this line of reasoning seems very

weak. He counters that someone could say that, although they die, still it does not follow that they sinned, since death occurs because of Adam, and for his sin they are rendered mortals. Additionally, does not Paul admit that the fault lies in nature when he proclaims that sin dwells in him and says that the law of his members drags him captive, and other things of that kind [Rom. 7:17, 23]?

But we will not allow Pighius to object that these struggles come from the basic building-blocks of nature. These building-blocks within us do not reflect a healthy and whole nature, but a corrupt and depraved one. Nor in this matter should he draw a comparison to brute beasts, since a human being is created to far excel the beasts and rule over them. It is true that people have in themselves the basic building-blocks to desire what is sweet and useful, but not contrary to reason and the Word of God. To have such impetuous and violent affections as those does not belong to human beings but to beasts. Second, our soul, since it is immortal and given by God, seeks a body that is suitable to itself, that is, one that can be kept forever, lest the soul be compelled to separate from it at some time. Therefore, we should not have recourse to the basic building-blocks of nature. What we have now is not the same as was placed in us at the beginning. But if Pighius imagines that God created those lusts and depraved affections in us, he will blaspheme and reproach him, which are the very same crimes he undeservedly tries to lay on us. Seeing that God is both the best and most wise and just, and that he created man for the utmost happiness, he would not endow man with things that detract from happiness. He would not commend the opposite of the divine mandates, nor that which is inherently vile; neither would he lead us captive into the law of sin and death. For, if these things must be put to death and crucified, as certainly they must, we must say that they are vices and hateful to God.

Nor is it a significant argument that he says that these things are not properly sins; unless, just as cold is called slow since it renders people slow, in that sense those things can be called sins because they incite people to sin; or just as Scripture is called a manuscript because it is written by hand, or language is called a tongue because it is carried out by its work, so also are these able to be called sins because they have proceeded from sin.[11] These comparisons in no way help the case of Pighius. Now, even if Augustine used to speak this way from time to time, still he intended it to be understood about those defects and vices which remain in a person after baptism.

---

11. In other words, Pighius argues that lusts and the like are not sins in and of themselves. If they derive from sin, then we can call them sins, but if a human being, acting on natural impulses but not sin, lusts, then that lust cannot be labeled as sin. For the analogy to which Vermigli refers, see Pighius, "De peccato originis controversia," fols. v^v–vi^r; and Augustine, *On Marriage and Concupiscence* 1.25 (NPNF, 5:274).

[CHAPTER 4:
CONCUPISCENCE:
A PROPENSITY FOR EVIL]

7. Keep in mind, however, that Augustine certainly considers these lusts and depraved affections to be sins even before baptism,[1] as does the Holy Spirit speaking through Paul, and the nature of sin properly applies to them [Rom. 7:5]. We have defined sin in such a way that it pertains to anything that opposes the Law of God. As John says, sin is transgression [1 John 3:4]. And who does not see that it is transgression that the flesh strives to subject the spirit to itself, and that our mind is unwilling to assent to the Word of God? Therefore, since all these lusts incite us to disobeying and rebelling against the Word of God, they are transgression and should be called sins. In addition, the words of David stand against Pighius's view: "Behold I am conceived in iniquities, and in sins my mother conceived

---

1. Augustine, *De peccatorum meritis et remissione* 1.24 (*On the Merits*, NPNF, 5:24); and *Contra duas epistolas Pelagianorum* 1.40 (*Against Two Letters of the Pelagians*, NPNF, 5:390).

me" [Psalm 51:7].[2] If these lusts and depraved affections were the works of nature, surely the man of God would not complain about them. And what else does the Apostle Paul mean when he writes to the Ephesians that we are by nature children of wrath [Eph. 2:3], unless sin exists in each one of us? Yet, Pighius tries to wrest this testimony from us with a perverse interpretation. He argues that the phrase *by nature children of wrath* only means *to be children of wrath*, that is to say, by a certain condition of our birth because we are brought into the world in this way. And he brings in the argument that some are called *servants by nature*, which means nothing else but that they are born in the condition that they serve. But we neither can nor ought to assent to this fiction, for the wrath of God is only provoked for just cause. It is not of the sort that it rashly or unpredictably becomes inflamed. For this reason, there must be something corrupt in our nature for the punishing of which the divine anger is stirred up. At any rate, his comparison does serve his intent. For, those who are said to be born servants by nature also have something in themselves that is suited to servitude. If we take Aristotle at his word, *servants by nature* are those who excel in bodily strength while being dull and slow in their rational capabilities. Thus, it so happens that they are more suited to serving than commanding others or living free.[3]

---

2. Pighius circumvents this argument by pointing out that "iniquities" is in the plural and so must not refer to original sin; see "De peccato originis controversia," fol. xviii[v].

3. Aristotle, *Politics* 1254b16–21. See Nicholas D. Smith, "Aristotle's Theory of Natural Slavery," *Phoenix* 37, no. 2 (1983): 109–22; Wayne Ambler, "Aristotle on Nature and Politics: The Case of Slavery," *Polit-*

The Apostle sufficiently explains why he calls us by nature the children of wrath. He says that we seem prone by nature to stir up the wrath of God, and we walk about according to the prince of this world, and in our hearts the devil is efficacious because of our disbelief, and we do the will of the flesh and our mind [Eph. 2:2]. These are the things that render us by nature children of wrath. And how can we deny that there is vice in our nature when Christ wishes us to be born again [John 3:3]? For, unless we are born corrupt, what need is there for us to be reborn? Besides this, in Genesis 8 [v. 21] it is plainly said that the imagination of the human heart is evil from infancy itself. And how will Pighius dare to say that what the Holy Spirit called evil is the work of God and a good thing?[4] To keep from appearing to speak empty nonsense, he invents that God said this out of his mercy, as if he wanted in this way to excuse human beings and to testify that he did not want to destroy the earth any more by water, because supposedly people are made this way and their thoughts tend toward evil even from their infancy. But in judging this to be an excuse, he is very much mistaken. Consider this

---

ical Theory 15, no. 3 (August 1987): 390–410; Paul Millett, "Aristotle and Slavery in Athens," *Greece and Rome* 54, no. 2 (2007): 178–209; and Donald Ross, "Aristotle's Ambivalence on Slavery," *Hermathena* 184 (2008): 53–67.

4. Pighius, "De peccato originis controversia," fol. xii[v]. At fol. xiii[r], Pighius goes on to argue that Adam's essential nature was not changed by his sin. On the Genesis passage, see Pighius, "De peccato originis controversia," fols. xvi[r]–xvii[r], where Pighius states that the flesh is merely brutish and thus incapable of righteousness or unrighteousness; it is just trying to fulfill its needs. The soul, however, leads it to sin because sin requires an operation of the will.

a better interpretation of this passage: that God wished to enter into a covenant with Noah that he would never again destroy the world with a flood, though otherwise people are such that they deserve it, and the imagination of their hearts from their very infancy is evil. These things do not excuse human nature from vice, but rather they mark out its sinfulness and corruption. Yet God in accord with his own mercy chose to spare mankind.

8. Finally, Paul tells us that through the disobedience of one man we were all made sinners [Rom. 5:19]. This shows that in those who are descended from Adam there is sin, whereby we are said to be sinners. But Pighius thinks he can maneuver around this because sometimes sinners are so called on account of their guilt, although the action of sinning has passed and no longer exists. Although this is so, still he is never able to show from Scripture that anyone is called a sinner without having sin in himself, or at least without having committed sin before—unless he means to say that God makes men guilty apart from any sin of their own. Second, Pighius does not notice that by his own fiction he introduces a vague, intermediate notion about the state of those who die only in the guilt of Adam. Yet the Scriptures teach us plainly that in the final judgment there will be no intermediate state; people will be committed either to the eternal fire or to eternal blessedness [Matt. 25:14–34; Mark 13:13; John 5:29]. It is rash to want to go beyond what is revealed in the Sacred Scriptures. Therefore, they are on a better path and wiser who leave this whole business to divine providence.

Still, it is worth looking at what has convinced Pighius. They will not experience any physical punishment, he says, because they did not contaminate themselves with a corrupt will in this life. How does this relate? It is enough that they had a depraved nature; they were prone to sinning, even though, because of their age, they were not able to sin. The pup of a wolf is killed, but who can excuse it just because he has not yet killed sheep or wreaked havoc on the flock? Still he is killed for a just reason, for he has a wolf's nature, and he is going to commit that violence if he is permitted to live.

To this Pighius adds another argument: that we are not required to have grief or contrition regarding original sin. What does he use to prove this? I ask, because all the saints groan deeply that this sin weighs down on them. David in his time, when he was in the throes of repentance, cries out, "Behold, I was conceived in iniquities!" [Psalm 51:7]. Paul so deplores this sin that he exclaims, "Wretch am I! Who will free me from this body that is subject to death?" [Rom. 8:24]. Although Pighius says that those who died in an intermediate state with only original sin will be content with their state, he offers no rationale except that, if they were to struggle against the divine will and grieve over the sentence imposed upon them, they would sin. There is no reason to suspect this of them, however, since in this life they did not sin. But here we have to ask Pigius whether infants had this right attitude or inclination in this life. He must deny it since they could not because of their age. Since this is so, why does he venture to attribute this inclination to them in the other life? It is much more probable that there they will incline toward evil, the seeds of which was here in them, than toward any good, of which they possessed no traces here.

The simile that he adduces about the generous prince, who not only manumitted his servant, but also lifted him to great honors, is not his own invention. He takes it from Aegidius, the Roman scholastic theologian, who nonetheless acknowledges with us natural corruption and depravity engrafted in us from the beginning. Nevertheless, we must examine it, lest, like a beautifully embroidered tapestry covering the blemishes of a wall, its appearance and loveliness conceal some error and perniciously deceive us. He depicts Adam for us as a servant, whom from the beginning God both set free and greatly enriched, so much so that he would pass on this wealth to his posterity should he obey God's command and Law. But if should fail to do so, he together with all his posterity would return to the original state of servitude. Herein lies the error of Pighius. He imagines Adam to be a person who from the beginning had a nature subject to corruption and bound to the servitude of the irrational affections. This is not true, for he was made by God perfect, so that he would not be like the beasts. Indeed, he had desires for things that were agreeable and which would preserve him, not ones that would rouse him against the Word of God and right reason. God gave him a body that would last forever. Therefore, when he sinned, he did not return to his original condition, but he invoked a strange, new misfortune upon himself.

For now, this will have to suffice as a refutation against this second opinion.

9. A third opinion is that concupiscence interspersed among the flesh and limbs is original sin. Augustine was of this opinion, as is apparent from his book *On the Merits and Remission of Sins* and from several other passages.[5] The

---

5. Augustine, *De peccatorum meritis et remissione* 2.45 (*On the Merits* 2.45, NPNF, 5:62).

Schoolmen interpret him to mean it, not only about the concupiscence of the lower parts of the mind, but also about the corruption of the will. But Pighius shouts back that Augustine held to the notion that only the concupiscence of the flesh and its members is original sin, as if Augustine did not mean that from the corruption of the affections, the mind is blinded and the will corrupted.[6] For, since these vices are all connected, he meant to include all of them. And he used the term *concupiscence* because in that vice the power of the disease shows itself more clearly. For this reason, Hugo writes in his work *On the Sacraments* that original sin is what we inherit from birth through ignorance into the mind, and through concupiscence into the flesh.[7] Lastly, when Christ says that no one can be saved unless that person is born again [John 3:3], he was not thinking only about the flesh or the part of the mind that lusts. First and foremost, our reason and will must be reborn. Afterwards follows the regeneration of the affections and the body, through which process all things are rightly subject to the Spirit and Word of God. But by the term *concupiscence* Augustine is not thinking of the act of lusting, but of the propensity, inclination, natural bent, and proclivity to the doing of evil. We do not always recognize these vices in small children unless, as it were, they betray themselves in time. Similarly, we perceive no difference in pitch black darkness between those who have sight and those who are blind. But when a light is offered

---

6. Pighius, "De peccato originis controversia," fols. vʳ–viᵛ.

7. Hugo of St. Victor, *De sacramentis Christianae fidei* 1.7.28 (*On the Sacraments of the Christian Faith*, 134).

or day comes, we can easily discover the impediment of the blind person. The wolf, before becoming mature, does not reveal its natural bent or rapacity. The scorpion does not always sting, yet it always carries its stinger for stinging. The serpent, while sluggish in the winter from the cold, can safely be handled, not because it does not have venom, but because it is not able to release it.

Moreover, Augustine says that concupiscence is passed on through procreation because all sinned in Adam. He thinks that the whole human race was in Adam *en masse*. And since human nature was corrupted in him because of sin, we cannot derive any nature from him except a corrupt one. We do not gather grapes from thorns nor figs from thistles [Matt. 7:16]. But he thinks that this concupiscence is inherited especially through the sexual act of procreating.[8] Yet some of the more prudent Schoolmen judge that, even though the parents are not engaging in lust during the act, nevertheless the offspring will have original sin because it was in the first man, in what philosophers call a seminal reason,[9] as it were. But if you ask of

---

8. Augustine, *De nuptiis et concupiscientia* 1.27 (*On Marriage and Concupiscence*, NPNF, 5:274–75).

9. *Seminali ratione.* According to Augustine, borrowing a doctrine of the Stoics and Neo-Platonists, this is the natural ability, power, or seed residing in things, implanted by God originally in the created order, that allows each thing to reproduce its own likeness. See Augustine, *Quaestiones in Heptateuchum* 2.21 (*Questions on the Heptateuch*, 95); *De Genesi ad litteram* 5.20.41 (*On the Literal Meaning of Genesis*, 171–72; see also Book 4, n. 67 and Book 6, n. 18). Also see the study of Jules M. Brady, "St. Augustine's Theory of Seminal Reasons," *New Scholasticism* 38, no. 2 (1964): 141–58, and the bibliography at n. 1; and Chris Gousmett, "Creation Order and Miracle according to Au-

Augustine whether he judges this concupiscence, which he calls original sin, to involve the will, he will respond that it can be said to involve the will because the sin committed by the first parents involved the will; in us, moreover, we cannot say that it involves the will, because we have not undertaken it of our own choice, unless, by chance, it involves the will simply because it is not put in us forcibly against our will.

Pighius attacks this point of view, saying that if the sin of the first person infected human nature, his specific sin must possess this type of natural effect. He would argue that there was nothing in that first transgression that had the power of infecting our nature more than any other sins. If it did, he thinks, we will need to admit that our nature is corrupted, not only by the fault of our first parents, but also through the sins of all our ancestors. Pighius considers it a very absurd proposition that those who are born later are more corrupt because they have more ancestors.

---

gustine," *Evangelical Quarterly* 60, no. 3 (1988): 217–40.

[CHAPTER 5:
THE REMOVAL OF DIVINE
GRACE IN THE FALL]

10. But the topic of whether the sins of all parents are passed on to posterity I pass over for the time being and will say at the end what seems right. Meanwhile, I reject his assumption about corruption being the natural effect of sin.[1] Corruption's origins can be explained by divine justice: through it, the grace of the Spirit and the celestial gifts, with which man was endowed before the Fall, were removed from him when he sinned. This withdrawal of grace was carried out by divine justice. However, lest you immediately retort that God is the cause of sin, that withdrawal must be blamed on the first man's transgression. For, as soon as God withdrew the gifts bestowed upon man, immediately sin and corruption followed of

---

1. Vermigli wants to argue here that it was not Adam's sin that caused corruption in the human race, but God's withdrawal of his grace after the sin. This allows him to explain how infants are born in depravity: since God's spiritual graces are lacking, they have a natural bent toward rebellion, which is wickedness or iniquity.

their own accord. These things formerly were alien to the human condition. Pighius asks how sin has the power of corrupting human nature—is it because of privation or something resulting from it? He thinks it is impossible that privation can corrupt human nature, since that is nothing and thus cannot cause anything; nor does he think it can result from that action stemming from privation, of which sort was the first man's wicked choice through his will. When Adam ate the forbidden fruit, he was not trying, nor did he wish, to corrupt his own nature nor that of his posterity.[2]

This argument is very weak. We see often that many things follow people unwillingly and unawares which, although they do not wish them, nevertheless are joined together with their actions. The person who intemperately gorges himself with food and drink does not do it to bring gout upon himself; yet, that is the result. In this way, though Adam did not wish for those things to happen, nevertheless when he sinned, they happened in and of themselves. But, Pighius says, since this lust or concupiscence comes about necessarily as a result of being born, and is not optional, we cannot hold the sinner to account or to blame. This results from his taking sin more narrowly and in a more limited way than he should. He wants sin to involve the will, and to be a thing said, done, or desired against the Law of God. But if he should take the sin as iniquity or wickedness, as John describes it [1 John 3:4], he would see that the nature of sin can be found in concupiscence. It is iniquity that the body does not obey the mind to do good things, and that lusts are resistant to the

---

2. Pighius, "De peccato originis controversia," fol. iii[r].

mind and want to dominate it, and that reason is opposed to God and shrinks back from his commandments. But since these things are wicked and unjust, whether they derive from the will or necessity, they are certainly sins.

But surely Pighius, who makes these objections, sees that he is forced into the position that the posterity of Adam are subject to his sin, but unwillingly so, an idea that is very much contrary to the Word of God. For, it is written in the prophet, "The son will not bear the iniquity of the father," and, "The soul that sins will itself die" [Ezek. 18:10]. This will certainly be false, if we believe Pighius, since children die and are subject to eternal damnation, though in no way have they sinned. We are not driven to this absurdity; we posit in all persons, as they are being born, sin and the reason why they will die and be condemned. It seems to Pighius to be an insult and blasphemy against God to say that he allows sin to be inserted into babies being born, seeing that they cannot help being born and affected in the same way as everyone else. But let Paul respond to this objection, who in this epistle says, "O man, who are you to talk back to God? Does not the potter have power over the clay to make from the same lump one vase for honor, the other for reproach?" [Rom. 9:20]. Let Isaiah also respond, who says that it is not fitting that a potsherd dispute with other potsherds concerning the work of their maker [Isaiah 45:9].

God does not have to conform to our standards and reasoning; but this would be the case if we were to measure his justice by the measuring rod of our judgment. Seeing that no day passes in which we do not complain and show our disgust about how the world is run, when will God be just? Who can explain why less grace is given to one who is perishing everlastingly, and more to another who is being saved?

11. I know that some say that God does not act unjustly in that regard because no law binds him to distribute the same and equal grace to all. But here certainly human wisdom will not remain content. People will complain and insist that he should be the same toward everyone, though not by the precept of human law but by the Law of his own goodness. Additionally, how can human wisdom see what the justice of God is, when supposedly some are taken away while still infants or small children, so that their hearts are not later perverted by evil and thus seek after salvation; while others live on to adulthood and earn for themselves destruction, though they could have been saved had they died in infancy? Here we must respect and admire the arcane things of God's divine judgment, and not want to correct or emend them to one of our prescribed laws. When the heathen Cato was siding with Pompey's cause because he deemed it to be more just than that of Caesar, and when in the end Caesar gained the upper hand while Pompey's supporters were scattered and put to flight, he looked up to heaven and cried out, "There is great obscurity in divine things!" For, it did not seem worthy of divine providence that Caesar should win.

And indeed, when I think on these things, I have to smile at Augustine's response to the Pelagians about this same problem. They had two objections against him that were somewhat subtle and difficult. One, how can it happen that God, who for the sake of his own goodness forgives our sins, wishes to impute to us those of another? The second is this: if Adam by original sin condemns us unawares and unwilling, why does not Christ save unbelievers so as not to seem inferior to Adam in any aspect? Augustine responds, "What if I were somewhat duller and not able to dismiss their arguments right away? Ought I therefore to believe divine Scripture less? No, it is much more fitting that I acknowledge my simplemindedness than charge the sacred writ with falsehood."[3]

But afterwards he dismantled both arguments. To the first he responds that God is supremely good and does not, as they allege about original sin, impute to us another's sin, but our own iniquity, which clings to our nature from the very beginning. To the second he says that Christ also saves those who are unwilling. He does not wait for them to become willing, but of his own accord comes to those who are sinners, unwilling, and resistant. He also leads to blessedness many small children who do not yet believe, nor can they because of their age have the faith whereby they might believe.

Therefore, I wanted to bring in these arguments to show that I may, if I wish, use the response that this father first used, and to say to Pighius this: Let us leave to God his own defense. He does not need us to protect him from being considered cruel or unjust. Let us believe the Scriptures, which proclaim in many places that we are born corrupt and tainted. Death also gives an indication of this to us, as well as all the troubles that we face. Certainly, God would not inflict these on the sons of Adam unless there is some sin in them that should be punished. But those who do not descend into themselves and do not contemplate

---

3. Augustine, *De peccatorum meritis et remissione* 2.59 (*On the Merits*, NPNF, 5:68); and *De Spiritu et Littera* 62 (*On the Spirit and the Letter*, NPNF, 5:111).

their own natural bent, how they are prone to all depravity, do not know what concupiscence means. Nevertheless,
not a few of the pagan philosophers did perceive it. They
marvel how in so excellent a nature can reside such great
depravity and self-love and lust for pleasure. And they so
recognized these evils that they judged that children need
chastising and punishment, and they urged them to correct this innate corruption through effort and exercise and
by undergoing hardships and severity. But they did not see
the real cause and source of these evils, which can only be
seen from the Word of God.

12. Pighius argues that this lust, which Augustine
calls concupiscence, is a work of nature and also of God,
and therefore cannot be seen as sin. But, as I responded
before, it does not come from the basic building blocks of
nature as instituted by God, but nature that has been corrupted. For, when he was fashioned, man was made right
and, as Scripture says, in the image of God. Therefore,
Adam's appetite for agreeable and preserving things, when
first he was created, was not raging out of control to the
point that he was averse to right reason and the Word of
God. That followed afterward. Therefore, we must call it,
not the work of God, as Pighius says, but the depravity of
sin and the corruption of the affections. For this reason,
Augustine calls the Pelagian Julian a shameless devotee
of concupiscence.[4] He, like Pighius, commended it as a
wonderful work of God. Besides that, Pighius also opposes Augustine for saying that concupiscence is sin before

---

4. Augustine, *Contra Iulianum Pelagianum* 3.26.66 (*Against Julian the
Pelagian*, 165).

baptism but denying that it is after it.[5] Pighius responds that the concupiscence is the same, as is God and his Law. Wherefore, he concludes that in both cases it must either be a sin or not. But Pighius errs greatly for two reasons. First, he is mistaken to think no change happens in regeneration, especially when he knows that Christ brings a remedy through the application of his righteousness and the removal of guilt. God does not impute the concupiscence that remains after regeneration.[6] Second, in the process of regeneration, we receive the gift of the Holy Spirit, who breaks the power of concupiscence so that, though it clings in us, it does not rule. This is what Paul is talking about when he exhorts the faithful not to let sin reign in their mortal body [Rom. 6:12]. On the other hand, Pighius is wrong to think that Augustine considers the concupiscence that remains after baptism not to be sin; he most certainly does, especially if it is considered alone in and of itself. Speaking with great eloquence, he declares that by its own nature it is a sin, which is disobedience, against which we must continually struggle. And when he denies that it is a sin, we should understand him to mean so far as guilt is concerned, since there can be no doubt that it is removed in regeneration. And so it happens that God does not impute it as sin, though it is a sin in and of itself. Finally, Augustine is comparing concupiscence with those sins which they call *actual*, and

---

5. Augustine, *De peccatorum meritis et remissione* 2.4 (*On the Merits*, NPNF, 5:45); and *De nuptiis et concupiscientia* 1.25 (*On Marriage and Concupiscence*, NPNF, 5:274).

6. In other words, after someone is reborn, God no longer reckons that person guilty for original sin.

by this comparison it can be said that it is not a sin, for it is much less grave than they are.

13. Furthermore, I marvel how Pighius dares to say that Augustine determines without the testimony of the Scriptures that concupiscence or lust is original sin, since in his disputations against the Pelagians he defends his position especially from Sacred Scriptures. And the reason he calls original sin *concupiscence* is because original corruption reveals itself especially through the crasser desires of the mind and flesh.

Now it is worth seeing what others have said about this. Besides concupiscence, some have the opinion that original sin is the lack of original righteousness. Anselm states this in his book *The Virgin Conception and Original Sin*, and he has convinced many Scholastic writers.[7] And by *original righteousness* they mean the right constitution of a person, when the body obeys the mind, and the lower parts of the mind obey the higher, with the mind subject to God and his Law. Adam was created in this righteousness, and if he had remained steadfast in it, we would all live in it. But since he fell, we have been stripped of it. They want to call this lack of righteousness *original sin*. But to explain more clearly their opinion, they say that not every defect is a bad thing. Although a stone lacks righteousness, we cannot therefore call a stone unrighteous or bad. But when a thing is fit and suited to have that which

---

7. Anselm, *De conceptu virginali et de originali peccato* 23 (Anselm, *The Major Works*, 382). For a discussion of this idea, see Aaron Denlinger, "Calvin's Understanding of Adam's Relationship to His Posterity: Recent Assertions of the Reformer's 'Federalism' Evaluated," *Calvin Theological Journal* 44, no. 2 (2009): 245–46.

it lacks, then a defect of this sort can be called bad, as in the case of an eye when it is deprived of the ability to see. Still, we do not say that there is a fault or sin in the eye. We only apply the term *sin* when the defect causes there to follow a struggle and contention against the Law of God.

Pighius condemns this opinion as well. He says that it is not a sin if someone does not keep the gift which they received. Sometimes a person who is born strong and healthy becomes sickly or maimed or disfigured.[8] No one would want to call these defects faults or sins. But this simile does not fit with the proposition, seeing that disease or mutilation of the body has nothing to do with observing or violating the Law of God. Furthermore, he contends that the loss of original righteousness is not a sin in small children, because they were not responsible for it being lost. But again, this is to call God into court. God is in a different class, and he must not be reduced to the rule of human laws.

But let Pighius compare his own opinion with that which he opposes. In the orthodox view, there is a vice and contamination in newborns that God condemns. Pighius, however, makes the children out to be guilty and damns them for the vice and sin that does not exist in them, but only for the sin that Adam, the first parent of all, committed himself.[9] In other respects, he thinks, those children are completely innocent. Which of these positions is more foreign to reason and adverse to human laws: that an inno-

---

8. Pighius, "De peccato originis controversia," fol. xiii^v. Pighius's review of Anselm's arguments begins at fol. vi^v.

9. Pighius, "De peccato originis controversia," fol. xxvi^r.

cent person suffer punishment because of another's sin or that a person is condemned whose guilt lies within himself? Certainly, to people who look at the matter closely, the opinion of Anselm in many aspects is better than that of Pighius. We know it is true what Ecclesiastes says, "God made man upright" [Eccl. 7:30]. But once he had sinned, immediately crookedness ensued. He no longer regards God and heavenly things any more but is continually bent toward earthly and carnal things and is bound to the constraints of concupiscence. That is what it means to lack original righteousness, since actions have not been taken away from human beings, but the power of acting well is removed. We all know by experience what happens in the case of paralytics. They move their hand, but because of the damage to their mobility, they move weakly and without control. The same happens also in us. When divine righteousness is absent, the foundational principle that we need for ordering and performing our works correctly is corrupted.

But Pighius says that the lack of this ability cannot be taken as a sin in small children, because they are not bound by any obligation or requirement to have it. He says if someone objects and says otherwise, they should explain what the law is that obligates the children. Since, he goes on to say, they cannot do it, let them cease to say that the lack of original righteousness is a sin. However, we will submit not just one law, but three. The first law has to do with the way human beings were created. God made man in his image and likeness, and therefore it behooves us to remain this way. God rightly requires in our nature that which he created. But the main reason for our having the image of God is so that he can adorn us with divine properties, that is to say, with righteousness, wisdom, goodness, and patience. But in opposition, Pighius exclaims that this is not the nature of the image of God. He says that it consists of intelligence, memory, and will, as Augustine in his *De Trinitate* and in numerous other books taught.[10] Indeed, the Schoolmen say this. But we will prove from the Scriptures and the Fathers that the matter is far different.

10. Augustine, *De Trinitate* 9.11.16 (*On the Trinity*, NPNF, 3:269).

[CHAPTER 6:
RECOVERING OUR
HUMANITY IN CHRIST]

14. It is written in the letter to the Ephesians that we should "put off the old person according to the prior conversation, who according to errant lusts is corrupted; but be renewed in the spirit of your mind and put on the new man, who was created according to God, in righteousness and the holiness of truth" [4:24]. And in Colossians 3: "You have put on the new man, who is renewed according to the apprehension and image of him who created him" [v. 10]. He then follows up explaining the properties of this image, saying, "Put on the bowels of mercy, goodness, modesty, clemency, gentleness, forbearing and pardoning one another" [v. 11]. And Romans 8: "Whom he knew beforehand, he predestined to become conformed to the image of his son" [v. 30]. All these passages sufficiently indicate what the Scriptures mean when talking about the image of God in the creation and origination of mankind. The Fathers understood this concept. Irenaeus in his fifth book says, "From the anointing of the Holy Spirit a person

is made spiritual, of what sort he was created by God."[1] And Tertullian against Marcion says that a person bearing the image of God shares with him the same emotions and inclinations.[2] His rationale is that man was made in the image of God at the beginning so that he could rule over creation as a kind of vice-regent, as it were, of God. No one can doubt that God wants his creatures to be governed well, for he constantly bids us not to abuse them; and the law binds us to ascribe to God, from whom all things flow, everything that helps us. But there can be no good use and right governance of things unless we are endowed with those properties that we have said belong to the image of God. Now, whereas Augustine situated the image of God in the intelligence, memory, and will, we say he did it to set before us a kind of example of the interaction between members of the Trinity.

We should not imagine, however, that he is saying that God made these faculties of the mind bearers of his image while being devoid of those virtues of which we have spoken. Therefore, we have a second law given to us, either from the institution or restitution of man, which Paul laid down; this law binds us like a bond, telling us we must recover the original righteousness that we lost. We also have the law of nature, and to live in conformity to it, as Cicero says in *On Ends* 3, is the chief and ultimate purpose of a human being. Moreover, this natural law depends on that other one we set forth. For, from nowhere else does it happen that we have thoughts in our mind

1. Irenaeus, *Adversus haereses* 5.8 (*Against Heresies*, ANF, 1:1316).

2. Tertullian, *Adversus Marcion* 2.16 (*Against Marcion*, ANF, 3:659).

accusing and defending themselves back and forth unless they are drawn from the dignity of nature as it was instituted by God. Whatever the philosophers or law-givers have commanded concerning the responsibilities of human life, all of it derives from the way we were originally created and formed. They could not derive those precepts for living from a nature that is corrupted by self-love and wickedness, the very things that make us prone to evil. They derive them from a pure and upright nature, the sort they imagine man's dignity provides us, but which we know from Sacred Scriptures was instituted by God and which we are commanded to renew. Some believe that Paul's passage about the law of the mind resisted by the law of the members applies here.

15. There is a third law that God wanted to have put into writing, "Do not lust." Although our adversaries twist this precept to make it refer to actual sins, nevertheless we have shown that it looks also to original sin, and God by that mandate wanted every kind of depraved concupiscence to be utterly cut off from men. Therefore, we now have laws which, so long as they exist, continually bind us and obligate us to perform that righteousness that they require. Yes, it is true that those laws are not understood by infants; therefore, in them sin lies dormant, as Augustine says in book two of *On the Merits and Remission of Sins.*[3] He follows Paul's saying, "At some point I was living without the law" [Rom. 7:9]. It is not that there was a time when the Law was not set over Paul; rather, during his childhood he did not understand it because of his age.

---

3. Augustine, *De peccatorum meritis et remissione* 1.67 (*On the Merits*, NPNF, 5:42).

Whence, Paul says, sin was dead, which Augustine interprets, asleep. But when this commandment arrived, that is, when he began to comprehend the Law, sin revived. No doubt, it was in him before sin. But since he did not understand it, it seemed dead.

Now it is apparent how the things that we said agree with Holy Scriptures. Yet still Pighius presses that these things in no way relate to infants, for the Law ought not to be set up about those things that cannot be avoided.[4] But when he says these things, he is not following the sense of the Scriptures, as they sufficiently teach that those things commanded in the Law cannot be fulfilled perfectly by us, though they are commanded with the utmost strictness. Paul says in this epistle, "What was impossible for the law, inasmuch as it was impaired by the flesh, God sending his own son…" [Rom. 8:3–5]. From these words it is crystal clear that the Law could not be performed by us as mandated. If it were possible, we would be justified by works, nor would there be any need for Christ to suffer death for us. There are other functions of the Law for which it is written. It is of course useful for directing the actions of the pious, but most valuable for pointing out sins. By the Law, Paul says, comes the recognition of sin. I did not know concupiscence, unless the Law had said, "Do not lust" [Rom. 7:7]. Additionally, by the Law sin is also increased and places more of a burden on us and oppresses us more heavily. For, "the law entered in that wickedness may abound" [Rom. 5:20]. And in Corinthians, "The power of sin is the law" [1 Cor. 15:56]. The purpose of all these things is so that a person, as if by a pedagogue, is led to

---

4. Pighius, "De peccato originis controversia," fol. vii^{v}.

Christ and seeks his help and prays that he might be given strength. By this, at least in part, with the first-beginnings of obedience, a person is able to perform what is bidden of them; moreover, that his failures be repaired from the righteousness of Christ and not imputed to him. Augustine, in book one *Against Julian*, censures the Pelagians because they imagine they have made a great discovery when they toss out the statement that God does not command what cannot be done. He teaches them the ends of the Law that we have laid out. Yes, Augustine himself in his *Confessions* reminds us of those sins that children commit even at their mother's milk.[5] Yet no one would say that they were able to resist these. Moreover, they were not sins unless they can be related to some law which they violated. It does not help Pighius or remove their sins just because they did not understand. Foul is foul whether we think it is or not. Anselm's opinion about the lack of original righteousness does not really differ from that of Augustine, who called concupiscence the original sin, except that Anselm says more expressly at times that which is covered more obscurely by the term concupiscence. But since this lack of original righteousness can be taken in this way, as if we understand only the privation of the gifts of God, apart from any fault of nature, therefore it is worthwhile to give a fuller definition.

16. Therefore, original sin is the corrupting of the whole of human nature derived from the Fall of the first parent and passed on to posterity through procreation, which, unless the gift of Christ gives aid, sentences all who are born in this state to almost infinite evils and eternal

---

5. Augustine, *Confessions* 1.6.8.

damnation. This definition contains all the categories of causes.[6] For the matter or subject, we have all the parts and powers of a human being. The form is the corrupting of all these things. The efficient cause is the sinful will of Adam, while the instrumental cause is the spreading of what is being passed on, which takes place through the flesh. The end and effect is eternal damnation, together with all the unpleasantries of this life. And the various terms used for this sin derive from these, so that sometimes we call it a defect, sometimes a corruption, sometimes a vice, sometimes a disease, sometimes a contagion, and sometimes malice. Moreover, Augustine calls it the affected quality and disordered mass. It is evident that the whole man was corrupted from the fact that he was made for the purpose of attaching himself to God as the highest good. But now human beings do not understand divine things; they impatiently await the promises of the Scriptures; they are bothered by hearing God's precepts; they hold in contempt his rewards and punishments; their raging affections petulantly assail right reason and the Word of God; the body refuses to obey the mind. Although we know these as native corruption through experience, even so they are confirmed by the testimonies of the Scriptures. Regarding the imperfections of our understanding, Paul says, "The carnal man does not perceive those things which belong to the spirit of God; no, he is not even able to do so, because they are foolishness to him" [1 Cor. 2:14]. In passing I will make the comment against Pighius that this passage indicates that some law exists that Paul cannot fulfill. This

---

6. He is referring to Aristotle's four categories of causes: material, formal, efficient, and instrumental.

particular law bids us to seek after and understand divine things. But Paul clearly says that the carnal man is not able to perceive these things. And so far as our design and purpose is concerned, we see that Paul teaches that this blindness or ignorance is engrafted and natural to man. For, it is unimaginable that it accrued through time or age. The more advanced in age someone is, the more and more he learns about God. From this we can see that people are carnal and unsuited to perceiving divine things because of their corrupted nature.

17. Of such great importance is this corruption that Augustine in *Against Julian* 3.12 says that it alienates the image of God from the life of men due to the heart's blindness.[7] He identifies this as sin itself, something that makes humanity's nature not quite in sync. Also, in *On the Merits and Forgiveness of Sins* 1.36, where he brings in the words of David, "Remember not the wicked deeds of my youth and my ignorance" [Psalm 25:7], he mentions the impenetrable darkness of ignorance in the minds of infants while they are still in their mothers' wombs.[8] They do not know why, from where, and when they were enclosed therein. The little one lies there unlearned, unteachable, incapable of understanding a precept, unaware where he is, what he is, by whom he was created, from whom he was begotten. All these things were incongruent to the nature of man as he was first created, and instead are corruptions of nature. Adam was not created like this; he was capable of under-

---

7. Augustine, *Contra Iulianum Pelagianum* 3.12.25 (*Against Julian the Pelagian*, 129). Augustine is thinking of Eph. 4:18.

8. Vermigli misremembers, because Augustine does not cite Psalm 25:7 here.

standing God's command and had the ability to name his wife and all the animals. But in infants we have to wait a long time so they can little by little dissipate this drunkenness, as it were. Additionally, that this ignorance should be considered sin is a contribution of Reticius, the very ancient bishop of Auton, as Augustine testifies in book one of *Against Julian*.[9] While speaking about baptism, he writes thus: "It is the principle indulgence in the Church, in which we expose all the weight of the ancient crime, and we wipe away the old deeds of our ignorance and put off the old man together with its innate wickedness." From these words we learn that our sins are inborn and that the sins of ignorance are removed in baptism. Wherefore, if we rely on Augustine's authority, since small children are baptized, they are shown to have sins, and that the old ignorance is removed in baptism.

Now, about the will, whether it also is corrupted, let us see. The Apostle gives clear testimony about it: "The sense and wisdom of the flesh is enmity against God" [Rom. 8:7]. By this sentence he includes all the affections of people who are not yet regenerated. But I marvel at the impudence of Pighius, who, in an effort to escape somehow, says this passage should be understood to be about the literal sense, which he contends stands in opposition to God and is unable to be subject to him.[10] The preced-

---

9. Augustine, *Contra Iulianum Pelagianum* 1.3.7 (*Against Julian the Pelagian*, 8).

10. Pighius is thinking about the Scriptures as having a *literal* sense and a *spiritual* sense, an idea developed at length by Aquinas. The literal sense encases the spiritual sense as the human body encases the soul.

ing and following verses clearly refute him, because Paul immediately adds a distinction between men who are in the flesh and those who are in the Spirit. From this we see clearly that he is dealing with, not the diverse sense of Scripture, but the variety of men themselves. The words right before that sentence were this: "What was impossible for the law, inasmuch as it was weakened by the flesh, God sending his own son in the likeness of sinful flesh, by sin condemned sin in the flesh, so that the righteousness of the law might be fulfilled in us" [Rom. 8:3]. These things also indicate that Paul is talking about us, not about the Scriptures in their literal or spiritual senses. In us is that infirmity whereby the Law is weakened so that it cannot lead us to salvation. And through Christ in us, the righteousness of the Law begins to be fulfilled.

18. Nor should we agree with those who in this passage and in many others want to understand it to be only about the crasser part of the mind.[11] When Paul gives an accounting of the works of the flesh to the Galatians, not only does he put adultery, whoremongering, and lust in that number, along with other similar things, he also includes idolatry, which no one can deny pertains to the mind, not to the flesh [Gal. 5:19]. And when Christ says, "What is born of the flesh is flesh, and what is born of the Spirit is Spirit," he is exhorting to regeneration [John 3:6]. This pertains, not just to the substance of the body or the crasser parts of the mind, but also and especially

---

11. By *crasser* parts of the mind, Vermigli means the lower, emotional part of the soul that can either be represented by baser impulses or, with the intervening aid of virtue, obey the superior part containing intellect and reason.

to the will and mind. And when he says to Peter, "Blessed are you Simon bar Jonah, because flesh or blood did
not reveal it to you," he signifies that he learned those
things, not from natural knowledge, but from the Spirit of God [Matt. 16:17]. The term *flesh* includes those
things which pertain to the mind and reason. But we do
not say, as Pighius foolishly mocks, that there is nothing
in the higher part of the mind but flesh. We know without Pighius's help that the mind is spirit. Nevertheless, in
the Scriptures it is called *flesh* when it is still in the state of
not being born again. The reason is this: when it ought to
be making the flesh (that is, the crasser parts of the mind)
spiritual, and rendering it obedient to the mind instructed by the Word of God, instead it caves in to its pleasures
and thus is made carnal.

Now they throw out as an objection what Paul says
to the Galatians: "The flesh lusts against the spirit, and the
spirit against the flesh" [Gal. 5:17]. They argue that this
cannot be possible if we do not leave anything healthy in
the minds of men. But we have an easy response to this
objection. First, Paul is speaking about believers who are
already regenerated, as the passage that follows sufficiently
shows: "So that you do those things which you do not
wish." With these words he is declaring that they have obtained a right will by the Spirit of Christ, which they are
not able to completely follow because of the constant conflicts of the mind and their great weakness. Therefore, the
Apostle in this passage wants only to say that whatever in
us is not perfectly regenerated struggles against the Spirit
of God. Second, we do not deny that there is some fight
of this sort from time to time in the unregenerate, but not
because their mind is not carnal with a propensity to sins,

but because in it are still inscribed the laws of nature, and because in it is some illumination of the Spirit of God. Still, this is not sufficient to justify a person or bring about a salvific change.

19. Additionally, Paul shows well enough that our reason is corrupt when he exhorts us to put on the new man, whom he says should be perpetually renewed in us [Col. 3:10]. Seeing that he thus wants a person to be completely changed, and that the person consists not only of the body and the affections of the flesh, but also, and much more so, of the mind, will, and reason, we have to conclude that these elements were also corrupted in the person. Otherwise, why did they need renewal? It is of no consequence if you say that we should understand these things to be about adults, who of their own choice and by their personal sins have caused corruption among these aspects of themselves. For, I ask, why universally did all the unregenerate contaminate themselves to the extent that no one is found among them who is innocent? He can say nothing to this question except that in them from the very outset these corrupt and sinful principles were in them.

Augustine also teaches we are regenerated only so far as we have been made like Christ. By as much as we are dissimilar to him, by that much we are not reborn, but retain in ourselves the old man. Let us see, therefore, whether from the very beginning we have a mind, will, and reason similar to Christ. If they are found unlike him, we must conclude that those aspects of ourselves are corrupted and pertain to the old person. Daily experience sufficiently teaches us the extent of the corruption of the lower parts of the mind.

Furthermore, it is characteristic of the lower parts of the mind that they be interspersed among the members and spread through all the parts of the flesh, which cannot happen with the higher mind and rational part since they are spiritual and indivisible. The body, it is clear, has fallen from its own nature so that it rebels and is averse to the mind. Paul teaches the same when he exclaims, "O what an unhappy man I am! Who will free me from this body of death?" [Rom. 7:14]. And again, when he says, "I feel another law in my members" [Rom. 7:23]. Finally, Christ's mandate for us to deny ourselves sufficiently proves that the whole man through and through is depraved. Now, if our nature were innocent and whole, there would be no need for us to deny ourselves, seeing that we must retain good things, not remove them. The lack of original righteousness fits our definition of original sin. Augustine's description also agrees with it, whereby he says that it is concupiscence of the flesh, provided that each is rightly understood. The chief among the Schoolmen, such as Thomas, Scotus, and especially Bonaventure, acknowledged this doctrine. They make natural corruption or concupiscence the material aspect in this sin; they make the lack of righteousness the formal aspect. And so they conflate those two opinions, which we have just now reviewed, into one. But some of our people want the formal aspect to be guilt or imputation of God. But since that is external to sin, I tend more to that opinion which makes the formal aspect to be the fight and struggle against the Law of God. That is the chief reason why the natural vices are to be called sins.

[CHAPTER 7:
ORIGINAL SIN IN INFANTS]

20. We should not listen to those who constantly cry out that our nature is good. We agree that this accurately describes our nature as it was created originally, but not so our fallen nature. Our nature has goodness but in such a way that it still has some corruption mixed in. And when they say that lust is good, they will excuse me if I give more credence to Paul than to them. He says, "I know that good does not dwell in me, that is, in my flesh" [Rom. 7:18]. And he adds, "I find by the law that evil is present with me when I would do good." He calls this concupiscence evil. To the Galatians also he confirms our nature to be sufficiently evil when he bids the same be crucified. It is also false what they say, that our nature always seeks what is useful and what preserves us. We experience its constant draw to what harms us and to those things that are detrimental to our life. Furthermore, if our nature were as innocent and good as they imagine it is, why does God need to punish it so gravely? Among all the living creatures, we see that almost none is as unfortunate as a human being, if we look at his birth, infancy, childhood, education, and disci-

pline. Everything is full of tears, grief, groaning, weakness, and labors. The body must labor for its livelihood, the mind is perpetually tormented with anxieties, the breast is stirred with strong emotions, and the body is afflicted with diseases. Some, when considering these things, have said that nature is not a mother, but a step-mother. I omit that sometimes the bodies and minds of infants and children are handed over to the devil to be vexed. Thus, we read in the Gospel that a boy was so vexed by the devil that sometimes he hurled himself into the fire, sometimes into the water. Therefore, divine severity acknowledges the innocence of nature in such a way that it gravely punishes it. Furthermore, it seems that the gentiles have been clearer on the matter than these theologians. Plato in the second book of *On the Republic* says that human beings are evil by nature: they cannot be induced to cultivate justice on their own accord, but only do so to avoid paying the consequences. And Socrates shows that no one exhibits virtue unless they are inspired by some divine power like the poets were. And Cicero in *On the Republic* 3 (as cited by Augustine *Against Julian* 4) says that a person is brought into the world by step-mother nature with a nude, fragile, and weak body, with a mind anxious about troubles, dejected in fears, feeble for its labors, inclined to pleasures, in whom lies hidden the divine fire, as well as natural genius and mind.[1] Ecclesiastical writers have arrived at this same opinion. Augustine collected their consenting opinions in *Against Julian* 1.

---

1. Augustine, *Contra Iulianum Pelagianum* 4.12.60 (*Against Julian the Pelagian*, 218).

21. We have already cited Irenaeus and Tertullian. Cyprian also says that Christ healed the wounds that Adam introduced, and cleaned out the venom with which the devil infected our nature.[2] Cyprian acknowledges the infirmity drawn from the sin of the first parent, whereby we are incited to sinning such that no one can flatter himself about his own innocence. Who can boast that he has a chaste heart? As John says, "If we say that we do not have sin, we seduce ourselves and the truth is not in us" [1 John 1:10]. Again, Cyprian in his letter to Fidus teaches that infants must be baptized lest they forever perish.[3] Augustine likewise cites Bishop Reticius, whose words we related above. He also cites the Spanish Bishop Olympius, who says that the vice of the first-formed man is so sprinkled among the seed that sin is born together with a person.[4] And Hilary writes thus about the flesh of Christ: "Therefore, when he was sent into the likeness of sinful flesh, so he had also sin. But because all flesh is of sin, derived from the sinful parent Adam, he was sent into the likeness of sinful flesh. No sin existed in him, but only the likeness of sinful flesh."[5] The same, while explicating Psalm 18, com-

---

2. Augustine discusses Cyprian's views at *Contra Iulianum Pelagianum* 1.3.6 (*Against Julian the Pelagian*, 7–8).

3. Cyprian, *Epistola 64, ad Fidum* (*Letters of St. Cyprian*, 109–11).

4. Augustine, *Contra Iulianum Pelagianum* 1.3.8 (*Against Julian the Pelagian*, 8–9).

5. Augustine discusses Hilary's views at *Contra Iulianum Pelagianum* 1.3.9 (*Against Julian the Pelagian*, 9–10). The assertion is less puzzling if we keep in mind that Vermigli has defined original sin as a predisposition for sinning once God withdrew his grace from mankind after Adam's fall. Christ's humanity was born in this same state as a fleshly

mends this sentence of David: "Behold I was conceived in iniquities, and in sins my mother conceived me" [Psalm 51:7]. Also, in his sermon on the book of Job, he says that the body is the material of evil, which could not be said at first creation. And Ambrose commenting on Luke says that the body is a pig-slough and the lodging-place of sins, but by the help of Christ it is changed into a temple of God and a holy place of virtues.[6] And against the Novatians he says that our beginning is in vice.[7] Furthermore, in his *Apology*, he points out that in his psalm of contrition David says that before we are born we are stained with contagion; and before we experience the light of day, we receive the original unrighteousness and are conceived in iniquity [Psalm 51:7].[8] And of Christ he says that it was fitting for him to feel none of the natural contagion of generation given that he would not have in his body any sin. David thus deservedly bemoaned both his own natural iniquities and the stain that begins in a person before life.

Ambrose also says this in his book *On the Ark of Noah*: "Whom therefore has he now called just, unless one free of

---

descendant of Adam, but because his humanity was united with the divine nature as its aid and support, Christ would not sin and so did not *feel* that inclination and rebellion in himself.

6. Augustine turns to Ambrose frequently as an authority. Vermigli has drawn most of these statements from *Contra Iulianum Pelagianum* 1.3.10 (*Against Julian the Pelagian*, 10–11).

7. Augustine, *Contra Iulianum Pelagianum* 2.3.5 (*Against Julian the Pelagian*, 59–60).

8. Augustine, *Contra Iulianum Pelagianum* 2.3.5 (*Against Julian the Pelagian*, 60).

these chains, one whom the chains of our common nature may not hold?" Also, he says in Luke's Gospel: "Through the washings of the salvific ministry, those small children who were baptized are cleansed from wickedness."[9] Jerome commenting on the prophet Jonah says that small children are subject to the sin of Adam.[10] And lest you think he is only speaking about Adam's guilt imputed to them, in Ezekiel 18:41 he underscores that not even a child of one day is free from sin. He also draws a connection to this sentence: "Who is able to make clean that which is conceived of an unclean seed?" [Job 14:4]. And Gregory Nazianzus says that the image of God will clean out the blemish of the bodily inundation.[11] A little later he says that we should reverence the birth, whereby we are freed from the chains of earthly birth.[12] And while treating baptism, he says that through it the stains of the first birth are cleansed, whereby we were conceived in iniquity, and in wickedness our mothers begat us.

22. Augustine came to the defense of Basil the Great when the Pelagians tried to make him a partisan of

9. Augustine cites this at *Contra Iulianum Pelagianum* 2.2.4 (*Against Julian the Pelagian*, 58).

10. Augustine, *Contra Iulianum Pelagianum* 1.7.34 (*Against Julian the Pelagian*, 42); Jerome, *In Ionam*, at 3:5 (*Commentaries on the Twelve Prophets*, 265).

11. Augustine, *Contra Iulianum Pelagianum* 1.5.15 (*Against Julian the Pelagian*, 16–17).

12. Augustine, *Contra Iulianum Pelagianum* 1.5.15 (*Against Julian the Pelagian*, 17).

theirs.[13] Basil argues against the Manicheans that evil is not a substance, but a mode of conduct contingent on the will alone. He meant this about those who have contracted the sickness of their conduct from their own will: this conduct, he says, can easily be separated from the will of those who are infected. If it cannot be separated, then evil is a substantial part of it.[14] Augustine agrees with all these things, for the Manicheans held that evil is a kind of substance and that it created the world. Against this, Basil replies that this evil has its existence in a good thing and that it was added to it through the will of the man and woman who sinned. The idea that it can easily be separated from the will he attributes, not to our power, but to the mercy of God. And we also live with the hope that there will be no vestiges of it, yet not in this life, but in the next. He does, however, acknowledge the existence of original sin. He bears sufficient witness to this conviction in his sermon about fasting, where he says, "If Eve had abstained from the tree, we would have no need of abstaining. Healthy people have no need of a doctor, but only those who are ill [Matt. 9:12]. We have become sick through that sin; let us be made well through repentance. But repentance without fasting is empty." By these words Basil has expressed his

---

13. This entire section on Basil alludes to Augustine, *Contra Iulianum Pelagianum* 1.5.16–18 (*Against Julian the Pelagian*, 18–22). The Pelagians resort to these arguments because Basil seems to be affirming that sin must be an act of the will and thus not applicable to children.

14. By *substantial* here Vermigli is referring to Aristotle's categories of being; the only category of being that is not contingent on something else is substance or essence. Evil, according to Basil, exists, but not in and of itself or as part of the essence of our will.

opinion that because of the sin of Adam we are not whole and healthy. Moreover, he cites the twelve bishops of the East who condemn Pelagius.

Origen should be added to this group, who, when he commented on that passage of Paul about which we spoke, said, "Death came upon all men," and that Abel, Enoch, Methuselah, and Noah sinned[15] [Rom. 5:12]. And he says that he will pass over other Fathers, because all to a man have sinned. No one is clean from filth, even if he lived only one day. But he speaks much more clearly in Romans 6 when he says that baptism must be given to small children by the tradition of the Apostles. The Apostles knew that all are born into sin, which needs to be washed away by water and spirit. And Chrysostom addresses human fear of and harm by beasts, though they were created to be masters of them.[16] This, he says, happens because of sin, and because we have shirked our responsibility and duty. And Augustine affirms that the nature of small children has fallen because the beasts do not spare them. The same Chrysostom, expounding that passage in Romans 5, says that sin, which exists through the disobedience of Adam, has contaminated all things. He says the same thing numerous times elsewhere.[17]

---

15. Origen, *Commentarii in Romanos* 5.1.20 (*Commentary on the Epistle to the Romans, Books 1–5*, 314–15).

16. From Chrysostom's *Homilia in Genesim* 9.11 and 16.4 (*Homilies on Genesis 1–17*, pp. 124, 209); cited in Augustine, *Contra Iulianum Pelagianum* 1.6.25 (*Against Julian the Pelagian*, 30).

17. Augustine, *Contra Iulianum Pelagianum* 6.4.9 (*Against Julian the Pelagian*, 316).

23. And yet it caused the Pelagians, and especially Julian, no shame to cite this Father for a witness.[18] In the sermon *On the Baptized*,[19] while recounting the many gifts of baptism, he says that those who are baptized, not only receive the remission of sins, but also are made sons and heirs of God, brothers of Christ, his co-heirs, members and temples of God, and instruments of the Holy Spirit. At the end he adds, "Do you see how many gifts are bestowed upon the baptized? And some think that heavenly grace consists in the remission of sins. But we have enumerated an abundance of gifts. Therefore, we baptize children, though they are not contaminated with sin, so that they can possess righteousness, holiness, adoption, inheritance, kinship with Christ, and membership in his body." Based on these words, Julian thought that Chrysostom rejected the idea of original sin. But Augustine says that his words should be understood to be about sin which the child committed of his own deliberation. No one denies that children are free from this sin and for this reason can be called innocent. In this sense Paul speaks about the two brothers [Jacob and Esau]: "before they did anything good or evil" [Rom. 9:11]. At the same time, there is no one exempted from Paul's statement that "through the sin of one, all men have come into condemnation"; and, "through the disobedience of one, we have all been made sinners" [Rom. 5:16].

---

18. Augustine, *Contra Iulianum Pelagianum* 1.6.22 (*Against Julian the Pelagian*, 27).

19. This work is lost.

From these words, it is apparent how cautious we need to be in reading the Fathers; sometimes we read in them that small children do not have their own sins, or sins proper, though they especially acknowledge that in them there is a corrupt nature, that is, original sin. But to have sins proper can be understood in two ways: it refers either to those sins that come of their own will and are committed of their own free choice (and for this reason the statement of Chrysostom is allowed); or it refers to their own natural vices, by which they are both contaminated and for which they are damned. These latter cannot be disconnected from small children, since they are in them when they are born, as David clearly proves. In this regard, Augustine noted that in the words of Chrysostom, which are in Greek, sin is used in the plural and not the singular, as Julian cited them. The passage in Greek runs like this: "Διὰ τουτὸ καὶ τα παιδία βαπτίζαμεν, καὶ τα ἁμαρτήματα οὐκ ἔχοντα." In Augustine's opinion, the word ἁμαρτήματα, since it is plural in number, fits best with sins that are called *actual.* And he adds that the older Fathers did not argue so much about the existence of original sin because Pelagian was not born yet to dispute it. Pighius should have weighed these many statements by the Fathers, especially since he considers them eagles who see things with a very sharp eye and always fly to the meat of the matter. But I think he considers them to be accountant chips, which are placed here and there for the purpose of indicating now a talent, now a half drachma, at the whim of the one calling the account. So Pighius sometimes wants the Fathers to have full authority, while at other times, if they do not say what he wants them to say, no authority.

Thus, sometimes he extols them as eagles, at other times he despises them as crows.

In this matter he seems to have contempt for the judgment of his Roman Church, which otherwise he is accustomed to make equal to God. For, the Church so acknowledges original sin that it does not deem infants who die without baptism worthy to be buried in a Christian cemetery; and it would have infants, when they are brought for baptism, to be exorcised of the devil, who holds them as his slave.

[CHAPTER 8:
PIGHIUS ON ADAM'S
ORIGINAL WHOLENESS]

24. Therefore, I do not say this to approve of those exorcisms or wish them to be retained. We must pray to God about the matter, but not in such a way that it seems we wish to cleanse a demonic person by a miracle. And since today no such gift exists in the Church, there is no reason why we should want to imitate it. Nor do we concede that infants who are not yet baptized are possessed by an evil demon. Innocent, the bishop of Rome who lived during Augustine's time, agreed with what we are saying when condemning Pelagius's view of original sin.[1] We ought not to diminish this original sin, otherwise we will diminish the blessing of Christ. And those who do not acknowledge this stain neither feel remorse for it nor do they seek a remedy from Christ.

Certainly, Pighius in this matter went further even than the Pelagians. They were only denying the propaga-

---

1. Augustine, *Contra Iulianum Pelagianum* 1.4.13 (*Against Julian the Pelagian*, 14).

tion of sin by Adam. But Pighius clamors that this notion is impious and blasphemous and a reproach against God. Again, they thought it was enough to say that infants who die unbaptized must be excluded from both the kingdom of Heaven and the punishments of Hell. But he imagines that they will be happy with a certain natural blessedness, and happy in such a way that they will bless, praise, and love God with their whole mind, heart, and might.

But now let us see how he tries to cloud his own definition. First, he says, these shadows and corruptions of nature are understood either as privations of God's gifts or as positive things. If you decide that they are privations, I understand what you say. But your contrivances are nothing but tragic names and empty terms. But if you want these things to be positives, since in the newborn infant there is nothing besides soul and body, which are clean and have God and nature as their origin, from what source, he asks, did these plagues enter that you talk about?

First, we respond that the privations which we posit here are not like negations that take away the whole things, as when we say that a Centaur or Scylla does not exist; they are the sort of privations that leave their subject maimed, useless, and deformed, as happens in the eye stripped of sight and in the trembling hand of the paralytic. Original sin resides in us in the same way. Indeed, the powers and actions of the mind remain, but they are destitute of all morality and therefore are depraved and corrupted. But Pighius constantly errs because he imagines that the nature of a human being possesses a certain natural wholeness to which were added those supernatural gifts conferred on the first parent. According to him, after the first parent sinned, those gifts were taken away and mankind fell into his first state.[2] But this is sheer fantasy, since the nature of a person was instituted by God just as it needed to be. Therefore, when the gifts were withdrawn, it became corrupted and marred. And since the nature of man strayed from its created state, it is in sin. Second, we say that original sin is not just this privation, but also it includes positive things, as a propensity to evil, resistance to the Word of God, and the like. Therefore, Bernard says that in the union of the soul with the body, it is as if the soul fell upon a heap of sharp shards or bruising stones. And among the Schoolmen, William of Paris,[3] in his work titled *Sum of Vices and Virtues*, adduces the following simile: the soul is sent down into the body like someone falling into the mire, both deep and full of stones, and thus sinks in, is made filthy, and is hurt. So, he says, from the original sin we have sunk into the shadows of ignorance, we are corrupted with lusts, and, so far as the strengths and faculties of our mind goes, we are wounded.

---

2. Pighius, in his desire to deny original sin, asserts mankind's inherent goodness or propensity to goodness even apart from the supernatural aids of the Creator. What mankind lost in the Fall, in his view, are extra-natural, extraordinary benefits, but nothing that relates to a human being's tendency to goodness. Thus, if an infant dies, there is no reason he or she should be punished.

3. William of Auvergne, Bishop of Paris (d. 1249). Vermigli is referring to a part of the *Summa de virtutibus et moribus* titled *On Vices and Sins* (*De vitiis et peccatis*). The passage in question can be found in William of Auvergne, *Opera Omnia* (Paris: Jean Depuy, 1674), 1:273.

[CHAPTER 9:
NATURAL KNOWLEDGE]

25. As for what Pighius says, that both the body and soul are good things and have God as their author, I agree. And when afterwards he asks how they are therefore corrupted, I answer with Paul that it happened by one man who fell, and that its spread is facilitated through the process of procreation (we will address this latter point below). His argument that body and soul cannot in any way be corrupted because they have God as their author has no basis in solid reasoning. Adults also have both a body and soul which are works of God, and which are continually preserved by his hands. But these, however, can be defiled and corrupted. But if he says their corruption results from human will and free choice, we will also respond that corruption can happen by other causes, namely, procreation and seed. Therefore, Pighius bases his argument from what is not the cause as if it is the cause.[1] He wants to believe that if peo-

---

1. He means that Pighius argues that corruption arises from human will and thus infants cannot have corruption, but Vermigli denies the premise itself. For Pighius's arguments against the possibility of sin

ple are contaminated, it cannot be so unless it is through their will and free choice. This is not true. Every objection arises from his stated inability to understand how depravity flows down to posterity, how it can happen that infants are bound by any law, and how the Law can legislate something that we cannot avoid. But, when the Scriptures say, testify to, and teach these things, it makes no difference how much Pighius either understands or does not understand. We believe many things that we cannot verify as absolute fact with our reason and senses. This does not mean someone should insist on our believing what seems good to them, under the pretext that our faith should accept them even if our reason cannot, seeing that God can work in ways that our reason cannot comprehend. My answer is this: first, what we believe ought to be shown from Scriptures; second, if we are not able to comprehend it, we should rely on our faith, setting aside reason.

Our definition is not meant to imply that there is nothing good among the pagans or in nature. We only say this, that this original sin would cause the destruction of everything unless God offered in the regenerate a remedy through Christ. In them also who are not regenerate, God is sometimes present and illumines them with excellent, heroic virtues that restrain original sin, keeping states and governments held together in at least some civil order. Socrates was unwilling to escape from prison when he could. Aristides, when he was driven into exile, wanted for his fellow-citizens to never fall into such a state that he would come to their mind. Phocion, when he was about to die

---

passing through physical seed from body to body, see especially "De peccato originis controversia," fols. xi^v–xv^r.

and was asked whether he wanted to send a message to his son, said, "Tell him not to feel vengeful for the wrong done to me." The Roman Republic boasted Curtii, Scipiones, Catos, men of civic goodness and lovers of justice. Even in people who were strangers to God, these good qualities were restraints on original sin and a depraved nature, lest everything be in upheaval, good laws come to ruin, and the light of nature, in a way, be extinguished.

[CHAPTER 10:
THE TRANSMISSION
OF ORIGINAL SIN]

26. Since we have confirmed the existence of original sin through testimonies of the Scriptures, have refuted the opinion of Pighius, and have rejected the opinion of those who think that original sin is only the guilt obligation contracted because of Adam's sin; and since we have applied the definition of Augustine that original sin is the concupiscence of the flesh, and of Anselm that it is the lack of original righteousness; and since we have proven our definition thoroughly and by many testimonies; now it remains that we pursue our third question: how does original sin propagate itself in respect to its conditions and properties, how is it abolished, how are the remnants of it in people who have been reborn, and what is the punishment due it?

Now, people hold varying views on how it is spread to posterity. The first of these concerns the propagation of souls, which we will show by the judgment of Augustine is less complicated than the rest, although not everyone accepts it. The second opinion, which Augustine holds, says that original sin is passed down through the lust and inordinate pleasure of those engaged in procreation. This means of passing on original sin has two problems: first, it makes procreation necessarily an evil, whereas procreation does not necessarily entail wrongdoing. And the Schoolmen themselves agree that the person who is begotten without the sinful affection of the parents will nonetheless receive original sin, in which case they say that it is enough that it was in Adam as the seminal beginning.[1] Another absurdity is that original sin consists only in the unseemly affection of lust, when in truth it encompasses, as has been said, the depravation of the whole nature.

Others think that God creates the soul corrupted, because it will be the part of a person that is execrated and put under the curse. But this is also rejected, because it seems to be at odds with the nature of creation for it to be called a contamination. Lastly, most people hold that the soul takes on original sin from its union with the body, which is already infected and corrupted by the parents. And so, if it is asked what is the seat of original sin, or, as they commonly say, what is its subject, we respond that it is located in the flesh as in the root and beginning; from that font it also possesses the soul and is extended thus throughout the whole person. Therefore, the seed is the instrument whereby this sin is handed down from the parents to the children. Pighius objects that defects cannot flow into offspring through seed, except perhaps those things that we see adhering to the body of the parents, as in the case of leprosy, epilepsy, and other diseases of the

---

1. This is the same as the *seminal reason* in section 9 above.

body. But, he says, nature does not allow sin to be located in the seed's very substance so that it can be passed down to the children.[2]

Here we respond that, first, it is not true that only the bodily diseases of those engaged in procreation flow to the offspring. We see that many mental conditions are spread to the children from the parents, such as intelligence, madness, ambition, affability, pride, and other things of this sort. To the other point, we do agree that an evil quality or corruption, which is passed on through seed, as it is in the seed, is not sin. But that does not mean, simply because it is passed on through seed as by an instrument, it does not have in it the means of sin. In the same way, the qualities we mentioned do not render the seed itself intelligent, gentle, or greedy, yet, when they have been passed on, they make the offspring such.[3]

27. Addressing whether God can be designated the author of original sin, it is commonly asserted that the deformity and unrighteousness which is in this sin derives from nature already corrupted. Insofar as this nature was created by God, it does not exhibit corruption. This is a way of maintaining that God is responsible for whatever good is in nature. But the evil in nature needs no efficient cause, in their view, since it is nothing but a defect. For, a lack or want of something does not need a creator; if it were created, it would then exist in that thing.

---

2. Pighius, "De peccato originis controversia," fol. xi[v].

3. Vermigli will concede that corruption passed through the seed does not render the seed itself sinful, but it does render the whole person sinful once passed on to him.

But this is not sufficient. We agree that God is the author of the subject or essence that has the defect. But we cannot agree with the assertion that the defect itself does not have an efficient cause. There must be something that removes or prohibits the completeness which is missing, and that withdraws the grace and gifts with which our nature was endowed initially. Therefore, we must assign this lacking or defect to God, who did not bestow a wholeness free from defect. He does this always according to his righteous judgment, though it is not always manifest to us. Scripture make it undeniably clear that God punishes sins by sins. But these are not inflicted by God in such a way that they are sins stemming from him, since whatever God does is incontrovertibly righteous and just. The punishments themselves, insofar as they are punishments, pertain to the nature of goodness; yet, insofar as they proceed from us, they are sins.

Now, we do not affirm that God himself, in and of himself, when he creates the soul, pollutes it. It draws the filthiness of sin from the sinful body, to which it is joined. But human wisdom finds this a difficult stumbling block, because people think that such a union should in no way take place. Accordingly, it seems as if someone put something precious into an unclean vessel. It also seems unjust that the soul, which has done nothing good or evil, joins with the body, from which it contracts the original stain. Indeed, they think, if this is how it happens, human beings ought to abstain from procreation, just as lepers are urged to abstain if possible lest they continue to infect human nature by reproducing. And, because the end to which man was made is eternal happiness, it does not seem right that the soul be placed in the body whence it is withheld from that end for which it was created. Just as it is not right that the soul, which in no way sinned, be punished in Hell, so also it seems wrong that it be united with that body in which it incurs, not punishment, as in Hell, but sin and the hatred of God, which are far graver, and, in fact, incur it in such a way that it cannot avoid it by any means.

28. These matters are so difficult and obscure that human judgment finds them unsatisfactory. Indeed, there are some consolations gathered out of ecclesiastical writers which soften and mitigate these objections to the point that they are satisfactory to pious minds, but not as much as human reason demands. They point out that the soul is united with an infected and unclean body for the sake of the whole world, that is, lest the race of humankind, which is the head, be absent from it. God does not neglect his duty; he does not impede the course of nature, but now that the body is made, he creates the soul according to his predetermined order; and he rather wills man to exist, although he is not born without corruption, than that he not exist at all.

True enough, he does not bestow everything that he granted at the beginning, yet from his mercy he concedes many things. Finally, he proposed the remedy of Christ our Mediator, by whom the sin we contracted is cleansed. This sin, before conversion, drives the elect to Christ, so that upon feeling the force of their own sin, they take the cure from him. Then, after they once are grafted onto Christ, they have this residual sin to wrestle with, so that in the end they can obtain victories and triumphs.

But, you will say, God could have saved the human race by another means so that it would not be wiped out, namely, if he had created another man pure and perfect. Adam could have been left without children, while all the posterity could have been procreated from that other man without corruption. There is no doubt that God could have if he had wanted to. But this means he would not have raised up the fallen, saved the lost, and redeemed the one who completely perished. God wished to show this form of goodness so that, despite the corruption, he might save from destruction whomever he pleased. For "he did not wish to bruise the shaken reed and quench the smoking flax" [Isaiah 42:3]. He wanted to bring forth Christ as another Adam, who would preserve his children as the other had destroyed them. These and other similar things caused Gregory to exclaim, "O happy offense, which deserved to have such a redeemer!" I would not be able to say these words easily, given that I see in that matter nothing that is not pitiable and lamentable. The fact that such a great salvation followed is owed to the goodness of God and not the offense of Adam, seeing that from his offense such great goodness flowed only incidentally as a result.

29. Although these arguments cannot satisfy the objections to the extent that human reason demands, as we have said, nevertheless they give some measure of an answer. The union of the soul with a corrupt body in no way brings about the destruction of the elect. In Christ both body and soul are restored. And just as the soul through the body is polluted, so through faith in Christ, which is in the soul, is it repaired together with the body. The natural order of things requires that an innocent soul, which has done nothing good or evil, be joined with a sinful body; otherwise, the body must be left without a life-giving spirit, and the world bereft of the human species.

But, if we want to find fault with God, there will be no limits or end. Infinite souls will complain that they were created unpredestined, a fact that they did not deserve. Many will complain that they were born of impious infidels and barbarous parents, and died at a tender age, because of which they were unable to learn about God. These complainers could dream up hundreds more excuses of this sort.

So far as procreation goes, we say that it is laudable when it happens in the context of a legitimate marriage. We must consider the human being who is generated—that is, the proper effect, as the Schoolmen say, and a human being truly in and of himself—to be a good creature of God; but the vice and corruption are adjoined to him as accidents.[4] And this evil has a remedy that is not available in the case of leprosy or other incurable diseases. Also, we grant that man was made for the purpose of attaining eternal happiness. And when someone objects that he is recalled from this end goal by the sin of the body, we retort that he is invited to Christ by the very same means. Lastly, we confess that it could seem unworthy that an innocent soul is placed in Hell, since there it has no hope of redemption. Yet once placed in the body, though corrupt, nevertheless it can acquire salvation and redemption.

---

4. In Aristotle's system of the categories of being, all aspects of being save substance are contingent on what he calls *accident*, that is, they depend on substance and cannot be separated from it. In other words, vice and corruption do not belong to the substance of what it means to be a human; a human can still be a human without having sin. The substance of humans, or what it means to be human, is good since it is that which was created by a good God.

30. Now we must offer reasons proving indisputably that original sin is spread by seed and reproduction. Therefore, we will show it from Sacred Scriptures, since many vociferously reject this position and think that it is all imagined. First, Paul says that sin entered the world by one man [Rom. 5:12]. Therefore, we must look at how all men stem from Adam and so are participants of his sin. Moreover, we can find no other avenue than by seed and reproduction. Second, as the Apostle says to the Ephesians that we are by nature children of wrath [Eph. 2:3], and as the physicists say that nature is the beginning of motion, we must have recourse to seed and reproduction. For, seed and reproducing are the beginning of motion and of our origin. But David indicates this more expressly when he says, "Behold, I am conceived in iniquities, and in sins my mother conceived me" [Psalm 51:7]. By these words he unmistakably teaches that sin is passed down through reproduction. Job says it even more plainly: "Who can make that clean which is born of unclean seed?" [Job 14:4]. This passage proves that the infected seed of our ancestors is unclean, despite what Pighius counters. But now let us consider the opposite, how that sin is taken away. Just as it was brought in by one man, so it is removed by one man. Moreover, just as sin is spread by Adam through seed and reproduction, so on the other side, in the vast array of things that relate to Christ, there are some things that work like seed. These are election (predestination), grace, the Spirit, the Word of God, and baptism. God uses these last two instruments to regenerate his children.

But if anyone asks whether the external Word or visible sign of baptism are completely necessary, we respond that the internal Word, whereby people turn to Christ and are restored, is altogether required, if we are talking about adults. But in small children, there is no place for either the internal or external Word. And, indeed, the external Word is the usual instrument whereby God calls adults to salvation, though in certain people he uses only the internal Word by extraordinary means. Thus, he called Abraham from his land, and instructed Adam without intermediary, as they say, without any outward ministry. We should in no way hold the sacrament of baptism in contempt, given that those who neglect it when they can receive it, do not attain regeneration. But if the opportunity is not afforded, it will not endanger the pious man and the one who is converted to Christ for him not to be baptized. And for this reason, the Fathers made mention of baptism, of blood, and of spirit. And Ambrose said of the death of the emperor Valentinian that he had not lacked the grace of baptism since he burned with desire for it, though he was not baptized.

31. Moreover, if someone should ask about the small children of Christians who die without this sacrament, I would respond we have to hope well for them. This hope relies on the Word of God, namely, the covenant made with Abraham, whereby God promises that he will be not only his God, but also that of his seed. Yet this promise is not so broad as to include everyone, so I would not be so bold as to promise sure salvation for each and every child who dies. There are some children of saints who are not predestined, as we read in the cases of Esau, Ishmael, and many others, whose lack of salvation is not due only to a lack of baptism.

Yet, while we live here on earth, there remains in the regenerate the remnants of this sin. In other words, original sin is not completely removed by regeneration. Guilt is taken away, yes, and what remains is not imputed to eternal death. But everything ought to be judged from what it is without qualification. Therefore, if someone asks us whether the remnants in the regenerate are sin, we will respond affirmatively. But when you read in some authors that it is not sin, you ought to understand that they are speaking about guilt. We will address this more fully elsewhere. I would add that in death this kind of sin is utterly uprooted and removed, given that in the blessed resurrection we will have a restored body, one suited to eternal bliss. Meanwhile, while we are here, the innate corruption of our old man is constantly being whittled away so that in death it will finally cease to exist.

So far, we have seen three things: how original sin is propagated, through what it is removed, and what we should think about its remnants.

[CHAPTER 11:
THE PUNISHMENT OF
UNBAPTIZED INFANTS]

32. Now let us speak about punishment.[1] Some of the Schoolmen believe that unbaptized infants do not experience physical punishment. The Pelagians think that they will only be banished from the kingdom of Heaven; they give no further details. Pighius adds this in addition: that those who departed this life with only original sin will experience a kind of natural blessedness; will love God with all their heart, mind, and strength; and will proclaim his name and praises. Although he does not dare teach these things as certain, nevertheless he approves of them as most likely. But, in his *De fide ad Petrum* and in a few other places, Augustine asserts that unregenerate children, if they die, will experience eternal fires. The Sacred Scriptures seem to favor this opinion since in the last judgment we see only two possible sentences; it admits no third place between saving and condemning. The Papists, though they

---

1. Of those who die in original sin but commit no actual sins, as in the case of infants.

think there will be Purgatory until the day of judgment, nevertheless posit no middle place after that day. And it is patently written that those who do not believe in Christ will not only not have eternal life, but also will fall under the wrath of God [John 3:36]. As long as we are alienated from Christ, we are called sons of wrath [Eph. 2:3], nor is there doubt that God punishes those with whom he is angry. Therefore, we will say with Augustine and the Scriptures that the unregenerate must be punished; but concerning the kind of punishment and the mode of it, we cannot give details, except that, since there will be various punishments in Hell (for the Scriptures themselves assert that some will abide more tolerably than others), it is believable that, since they did not add actual sins to their original sin, they will be punished more lightly. Yet, I always except the children of the saints, because we do not hesitate to count them among believers, although they do not in reality believe yet because of their age. We do not reckon the children of infidels among believers, though in and of themselves they are not rejecting the faith. From this, believers' children who have died without being baptized, because of the covenant that God struck with the parents, can be saved, if they are predestined as well. I except any others too who are predestined by the hidden counsel of God.

[CHAPTER 12:
GENERATIONAL GUILT]

33. Now that we have laid this foundation, let us come to
the arguments of the Pelagians whereby they thought that
they could prove that there is no original sin. First, they
argue that it is not likely that God wishes still to prosecute
the sin of Adam when he already did so once sufficiently,
especially since Nahum the prophet says that God will not
judge twice for one and the same thing [Nahum 1:9]. I
know that some respond that God did not pass judgment
on that sin twice, but only once, for in one judgment is
included the sin of Adam and all his progeny. But to explain the matter more plainly, I say in each one of us there
is reason why we are punished each time we are punished.
Therefore, everyone pays the penalty for his own sin and
not that of someone else. But, if we read that God punishes in us the sin of Adam, we must understand that it is
because our wrongdoing has its source from him. It is as
if someone suffering from the plague infects others and
those others die; we would say that each person died from
his own sickness and not from that of someone else. But,
if someone says those others died from the plague of that

one from whom they contracted the contagion, this must be taken to mean that this person first came upon the plague and communicated it to them.

Furthermore, that statement of Nahum the prophet does not relate to this. Indeed, Jerome, when interpreting this passage, says that these words refute Marcion, who was accusing the God of the Old Testament for seeming vengeful and cruel because he meted out very harsh punishments. Jerome ascribes this, not to cruelty, but to goodness. God punished people so harshly in Sodom, in the flood, and in other instances, for no other reason than that they might not perish everlastingly. Once he avenged himself on them, never again did he chastise them. But the same Jerome, perhaps because he realized that these things were not on solid footing, reconsiders. One could take from this that it is a good thing if adulterers are caught, for in this way it comes to pass that, while they suffer capital punishment, they avoid the eternal punishments of Hell. Wherefore, he responds that the judge of this world is not able to preempt the judgment of God; nor must we think that sins that deserve a heavy and eternal penalty can be removed by light punishment.

In these words of Jerome we should observe two things: one, that during his day adultery was a capital crime; second, that the first interpretation does not seem to be sufficient for him. Therefore, he adduces another explanation of the Jews, that God by these words wanted to indicate that the Assyrians, after enslaving ten tribes, would not gain power also over the kingdom of Judah, as they tried under Hezekiah. God, he says, will not permit a double jeopardy to arise. He considers it sufficient to have destroyed ten tribes; he wills that the kingdom of Judah remains safe.

Although this exposition is in no way impious, nevertheless it does not seem to agree with the prophet's intent. He prophesied against Nineveh the threats of God and the future destruction. And when he was of a mind to exaggerate the impending judgment, he says that such great violence of devastation will be visited upon them through the Chaldeans that it will not be necessary for the Lord to inflict punishment on them again; that by the first punishment he will exact a sufficient penalty. Thus, the empire of the Assyrians was utterly overturned by the Chaldeans. And we often say of a man who is beaten to death that he was so struck by one blow that there was no need for a second. This is the intent of the prophet and the real sense of this passage.

Moreover, as far as the matter is concerned, we do not deny that afflictions in godly men have in view what Paul says, "that they not be condemned with this world" [1 Cor. 11:32]. They are paternal corrections whereby the godly are recalled to penitence. We must not take a general rule from it, however, whereby a restraint is imposed on God so that when he begins to punish the ungodly in this life, he cannot also punish them in the next if they die outside of the faith and repentance. If they return to God, they do not suffer in the next life; nevertheless, this is not because in this life they gave satisfaction to God through the penalties that they paid, but because Christ on their behalf paid off the price of their redemption. Wherefore, just as certain good things are given to the godly in this life, which are for them pledges and the beginnings of a life to be enjoyed in another time, so in the ungodly eternal punishments have their beginning in the preliminary afflictions of this life. Even Christ seems to insinuate this when he says, "Fear the one who is able both to kill the body and send the soul to Hell" [Luke 12:5]. From these words I think it is sufficiently clear that the pronouncement of the prophet, which we have plainly expounded, relates not at all to the matter at hand.

34. Another one of their arguments is taken from the prophet Ezekiel: "The son will not bear the iniquity of the father" [Ezek. 18:20]. We can respond to this in one word, as we said a little ago: namely, that children do not bear the iniquity of their parents, but their own, personal iniquity, which clings to each person from birth. But, since different people explain the passage in different ways, we will lay out what we think it means. The Jews frequently used to pass around a proverb that runs something like this: "Our parents ate sour grapes, and the teeth of the children pucker."[1] Ezekiel is not only mindful of this proverb, but also Jeremiah 31 [v. 29]. The meaning of this saying is this: Our parents have sinned, and we pay the price for them. As the Rabbis say, those who were of the kingdom of the ten tribes seemed to relate these things to Jeroboam the son of Nebat, who first made the golden calves. They who were from the kingdom of Judah were relating these same things to Manasses, for whose impiety they were thinking that captivity would fall upon them, as the prophets were threatening would happen.

God reproves this proverb and says that it will not be so hereafter. "The souls are mine," he says; "The child

---

1. Pighius also discusses this saying at "De peccato originis controversia," fols. xxviii[r-v].

will not bear the iniquity of the father, but each one will die in his own sin." Many consider this to be about civil punishment, since in Deuteronomy 24 [v. 16] God commanded that neither should the parents die for their children nor the children for their parents. Amaziah, the king of Judah, also observed this, as 2 Kings 14 relates. He killed the assassins of his father, but he spared their sons in accord with the precept of the Law. However, the Israelites did not always observe this. In the seventh chapter of Joshua we read that, not only was Achan killed for taking something that was forbidden, but also along with him his sons, daughters, and cattle. But this was done in accord with a singular command of God and should not prejudice the Law given in general.

35. Nevertheless, this exposition concerning the civil law does not square with the words of the prophet. The Jews were not complaining about punishment imposed on them by the courts or inflicted on them by their ruler, but about those calamities that God himself visited upon them, namely, the devastation of their property, the overthrow of the Judaic kingdom, and the Babylonian captivity. Here they were pointing the finger at the judgments of the Lord and they were murmuring that his way is not right.

Therefore, some have interpreted this passage to be about eternal punishments, the loss of grace, and the loss of the Spirit. They agree that these things befall each individual as a result of his own sins and not for the sins of others. Yet, at the same time, they assert that children suffer temporal punishments because of their parents and the people because of their leaders. God, they say, wills to punish the parents in their children, since the children are a certain part of the parents. And they say that it is not absurd if the children by their afflictions benefit the parents, since in this way they themselves are recalled to repentance, and since no harm comes to themselves if they die, given that they are mortal. God wisely dispenses the times of living and dying and, they say, he snatches the children from life so that they not be corrupted by evil or, if they are already immersed in sinned and are damned, so that they not be burdened even more, seeing that they put an end to their bad living. Augustine seems somewhat inclined to this opinion in his *Questions on Joshua*, questions 8 and 9.[2] Those who assert that the remains of original sin lingering after regeneration are not sins, are forced to maintain this since they cannot say that in small children their own sins are punished, given that they hold there are none. But we, who say that these are most certainly sins, teach that they are not imputed to eternal death, but nevertheless sometimes result in punishments, so that we can understand that they are displeasing to God."

But, not even this exposition of Augustine meshes well with the sense of Ezekiel. The prophet says that it will not come to pass that the children will say that they are suffering temporal punishments, such as exile and captivity, because of their parents. The Lord says, "The son will not bear the iniquity of the father." Therefore, it in no way mitigates those things for some to say that this is true

---

2. Vermigli is referring to one part of the larger *Questions on the Heptateuch* (*Questionum in Heptateuchum libri septem*), specifically the section on Joshua (book 6) bearing the title "Quaestiones in Iesu Nave" (Questions on the Birth of Jesus). There he talks about how the Israelites suffer for Achan's theft, that is, for the sins of another, yet at the same time the Lord knows each individual's heart.

in spiritual punishments and in eternal damnation. The prophet quite clearly is speaking about the bodily punishments of this life. Augustine put forward another interpretation at *Enchiridium to Laurentius* 46, stating that this is a prophecy about the benefits conferred through Christ. For, given that he made satisfaction through his death for original sin, the prophet says that after this the child will bear, not the sin of the parent, but his own. Augustine seems led into this opinion because, when Jeremiah in chapter 31 is writing almost the same thing, immediately there follows a promise of the New Testament. "Behold," he says, "the days are coming when I will strike a new covenant with the house of Judah." But not even this interpretation seems to agree with the prophet's meaning that we related before. And again, although Christ suffered in a fixed time, nevertheless, by the power and grace of his death, children in the Old Testament also were saved. Additionally, they who are outside Christ bear their own iniquity, nor do they pay the penalty for another's sins, only their own.

In light of these difficulties, we hold that the statement of the prophet is generally true: all children or adults, both of the Old and the New Testament, bear their own iniquity. All who are born have sin and corruption in themselves for which they deserve punishment. Wherefore, this statement confirms our opinion; it is far from being a refutation against us. But it does undercut Pighius, who maintains that children bear the sins of their parents, since otherwise they are clean and born without sin. The Jews were proclaiming that they were innocents; moreover, they complained that the punishments that they were suffering were for the sins of their parents. Their parents had

sinned, they were saying, not they. But God says that hereafter there will be no place for this proverb. He was want-
ing through the prophet to declare the fuller illumination
of the Holy Spirit that would come in the New Testament.
His judgments are not such that he should punish any
innocent person for the sin of another. Therefore, he does
not say that it will not be so hereafter, as if it ever was
before. But he says this: it will not come to pass that they
can have recourse to a proverb of this sort since they will
finally know the truth.

36. But the Law seems to stand against this exposition, for in it God says that he visits the iniquity of the
fathers against the sons unto the third and fourth generation [Exod. 20:5]. These two ideas do not seem to agree,
the one that God visits the iniquity of the parents on the
children, and the other that the children do not bear the
sins of their parents. To satisfy this objection, let us ex-
pound upon the words of the Law. By this means we will
come to understand that there is no tension between the
statements in the Law and the prophet.

Some refer the sentiment expressed in the Law to the
mercy of God, others to his severity and justice. Those
who think that the mercy of God is commended by these
words say that God is so good and kind that he does not
immediately want to destroy people when they sin, pre-
ferring instead to await their repentance. Therefore, sometimes when he spares the parent who has sinned, nevertheless he punishes the child. Sometimes when he spares the
parent and the child, he chastises the grandchild; at other
times he defers the punishment into the fourth generation. This is the case with King Jehu of Samaria [2 Kings
15:12]. Although he sinned grievously, still God did not

take away the kingdom from his posterity until after the fourth generation. It seems, therefore, that these words proclaim God's goodness. He restrains his anger thus and does not immediately pour it out.

But others think God's goodness is proclaimed when it is said that he will bless those who love him for a thousand generations. In contrast, to reveal his strictness and justice, it is added that he will persecute sins not only against those who have sinned, but also against their children and grandchildren up to the fourth generation. They think there are examples to demonstrate this. Amalek inflicted numerous troubles upon the Israelites while they wandered through the desert, and after a long interval the Israelites did the same to his posterity, so much so that in the end God bid Saul to wipe them off the face of the earth [Exod. 17:8; 1 Sam. 15:2]. Another example is represented in Gehazi, the servant of Elisha, who, because he had received money in his master's name from Naaman the Syrian, himself was struck with leprosy and all his posterity after him [2 Kings 5:27].

Each of these sentiments is pious and can be confirmed by examples, but the latter seems to square better with the text. Just how God visits the iniquity of the parents to the children unto the third and fourth generation, the Law itself declares well enough from the added statement, "those hating me." From this it is apparent that only the children who are like their parents will bear their sins. If they depart from their wickedness, they will not bear their sins. And it must be noted that the phrase, "those hating me," should be taken in two ways: either in action, as they say, which only fits with the adults, or else by the inclination and corruption already conceived by nature, which takes place in children.

37. Someone might object that if we think God only punishes those who imitate the sins of their elders, why was it necessary to add the phrase, "unto the third and fourth generations"? In every generation God punishes all sinners regardless of who they are. This objection caused Augustine to explain that by the rhetorical expression, "unto the third and fourth generations," we must understand "to all posterity." A finite number is being used to express infinity. If you add the number four to three, you get seven, which often stands for another number, whatever that might be. He points to a similar expression in the prophet Amos: "For three offenses and for four I will not reverse his course" [Amos 1:3, 6, 9]. And this is his feeling about this passage: If someone transgresses once and then again, God can forgive him. But if someone heaps sins upon sins without measure, now God cannot forgive him. These "three or four offenses" stand for the continuance of sins. Also, in this way God can be said to punish unto the third and fourth generation of those who hate him, since against all such ones as these, whoever they are, he is going to exact punishment.

But there is a different possibility, namely, that God chose the third and fourth generations as the limit for the tempering of his wrath with mercy, and at some point put an end to his punishments, no longer continuing with them. However, there are some who think that the third and fourth generations are specified on purpose, because it is this far that the descendants are induced to follow the evil example of their progenitors. The idea is that none of the elders are still living: generally speaking, they die after seeing the fourth generation.

From these things we see that the words of the prophet in no way contradict the Law but rather interpret it. Therefore, he says that the child will not bear the iniquity of the parent because the Law says that the sin of the parents visits the children if they also imitate the sins of the parents.[3] Thus, they understand, when they are punished, they are paying the price for their own sins, not of the parents. Moreover, God is said to punish the sins of the parents in them because the sins took their beginning in them and were continued unto the children. But if the children did not have parents or grandparents who had so sinned, perhaps God would stay his wrath at this point, and as he showed patient restraint with the progenitors, so also perhaps he would show the same to them. But when the progenitors have sinned, and the descendants do not refrain from following their example, God will not defer his punishment any longer, lest he seem to have cast off the care of human affairs, causing others to sin due to his lack of concern.

At the same time, those who are so punished cannot be called innocent, since they themselves also hate God. Nor is there a contradiction that Christ says to John concerning the man blind from birth, "Neither he sinned nor his parents." Now, this passage does not mean that the blind man was punished undeservedly. It only indicates

---

3. For the discussion of this solution to the problem of paternal sins in the twelfth century, see Artur Michael Landgraf, "Die Vererbung der Sünden der Eltern auf die Kinder nach der Lehre des 12. Jahrhunderts," *Gregorianum* 21 (1940): 203–47.

this, that the providence of God directed his blindness to another end than that the man be punished. He willed it so that on that occasion he could demonstrate the divinity of Christ. Thus, God distributes punishments so that he might not only punish by means of them, but also accomplish other ends that he himself has laid down. And this is what we can say about the passage of the prophet. From these arguments it can be understood that he is not at odds with either the Law or any definition brought to bear by us. No, rather, such a sentence must be turned against our adversaries, who assert that the children are subject to the sin of another.

[CHAPTER 13:
GODLY PARENTS
AND INHERITED SIN]

38. The next reason was this: since both the soul and body are works of God, since progenitors often are holy and pious and the Scriptures commend them, and since the Scriptures praise the act of procreation and marriage, how, among so many fortresses of innocence, did sin work its way in?

We respond with Paul, "through one man." Their assumption that the progenitors were clean and holy is false. For, though they were endowed with piety and their original sin forgiven, so far as guilt goes, still there remains in them a corrupt nature and an impure state. Therefore, they pass down the sort of nature that they have in themselves to their posterity, and they do so, as has been said, through seed and generation.

Now, that the body is not able to act on the spirit does not present an obstacle, as they imagine. We do not say that the spirit is corrupted by the body or physical action. But, seeing that the body is corrupted, it resists the soul, and the soul, no longer strengthened with its original endowments, is subject to the body's inclination. Nor does it rule the body, as it was equipped to do, but is ruled by it.

Additionally, natural processes teach us that there is a cooperation between body and soul, since the soul is variously affected by the temperature of the body. Those who have an excess of yellow or black bile are often angry or sad. Therefore, seeing that this argumentation starts from false principles, it can conclude nothing. Additionally, a passage was brought up from 1 Corinthians: "Your sons are holy" [1 Cor. 7:14]. Therefore, the argument goes, it is not likely that they inherited original sin, since that holiness does not fit with sin. Some explain here that the children of Christians are holy in regard to civil law, meaning they are lawful children and not bastards. But this does not hold, because the marriage of Christians is not different from the marriage of infidels before the law. The children of legitimate marriages are themselves considered legitimate and heirs. Others interpret *holiness* to stand for *pious education*, arguing that if a pious spouse separates from an impious one, perhaps the children are left with the impious partner and are thus led away from Christ. But if the spouses live together, the pious parent will always instill some measure of piety in the children. But not even this seems to relate much to what Paul is teaching, because even the children born of adultery or prostitution can receive a pious education. We see this in the case of Augustine's son Adeodatus.

Therefore, the Apostle seems instead to indicate that something of the pious parents' holiness redounds to the children. This, however, does not stem from the flesh, but from the promise given in the covenant. God promises to

Abraham that he intends to be, not only his God, but the God of his seed [Gen. 17:7; 2 Cor. 6:18]. Therefore, in the prophets God calls the children of the Jews his own and complains that they are sacrificing his sons and daughters to Moloch [Ezek. 16:20–21]. We, relying on this hope of the promise, offer our children to be baptized in the Church, because they belong to God and Christ, so that the promise, which we just now mentioned, might be confirmed by an external sign.

39. But you will say, "You can be deceived. Perhaps your child will not belong in the number of the elect." I respond that the same difficulty applies to adults. It is possible that someone feigns a profession of faith;[1] or is brought to the fold only by human persuasion; or has faith for only a time, so that he does not really belong among the elect. But a minister does not look to those things, but only to the confession of the person who is about to be baptized. He understands that God's election is hidden from him and therefore is not his concern. He cannot determine anything about particulars but attends to the general promise. Although many are excluded from it, nevertheless it is not his role to decide who they are. Paul speaks thus concerning the Jews: "If the roots are holy, the branches are also; if the first-fruits are holy, so is the whole batch or lump of them" [Rom. 11:16]. By these words he shows that God's favor was inclined to the Jews because of the promise and because of their forefathers; for that reason, salvation was due to them. So, even though

1. On this issue in the tradition, see Marcia Colish, *Faith, Fiction, and Force in Medieval Baptismal Debates* (Washington, D.C.: The Catholic University of America Press, 2014).

this promise is indefinite, and many are excluded from it, nonetheless it remains unshaken. Some of them are always converted to Christ and will continue to convert to the end. This truth is apparent in the case of Isaac. God promised that he would show favor to his seed, but this was fulfilled only in Jacob, not in Esau. Still, this did not keep Esau from being circumcised.

Thus, we affirm that the children of Christians who belong to the number of the elect are holy; nevertheless, they are polluted with original sin, because by nature they are children of wrath like the rest. But if God suspends their guilt and does not impute it to them against their salvation, they have it by the grace of God and his pure mercy, not from the purity of their own nature. Therefore, since they are born from a corrupt mass and are among the elect, we can affirm two things: they are holy, and they are by nature children of wrath. This is how we must resolve this topic.

But they add that infants say, do, or think nothing against the Law of God, and therefore they have no sin. The unseemly nature of their error is apparent from what we just said. It is as if they are saying, "They do not have actual sin; therefore, they have no sin." To argue from the species to the genus through negation is the worst kind of logic.[2] They make their mistake in not following the universal nature of sin which I described above, that it encompasses everything that in any way is contrary to the Law of God.

---

2. This belongs to the technical terminology of dialectic. He is saying that actual sin is a subcategory or particular kind (species) of the general category (genus) of sin.

[CHAPTER 14: AGGREGATED GUILT]

40. They object, saying that it is incorrect to say that original sin is propagated through seed and flesh, because these things are by nature senseless and animalistic, and therefore lack the capacity for sin. But, I have already said that sin is not in them except by their origin, as in the root. Sin's nature is made complete, however, once the soul is joined to it. We explained also how to counteract the arguments of the Pelagians when they contend that what Paul says in this passage should be understood in terms of imitation. This does not agree with Paul's statements elsewhere. He says, "All have sinned, and through the disobedience of one many were made sinners" [Rom. 5:19]. And what is even firmer, he teaches, "Thus, before the Law sin was in the world, because death ruled from Adam to Moses" [Rom. 5:14]. There were also other arguments which Augustine uses against the Pelagians that we do not need to repeat here.

Furthermore, they add that human affliction and death itself are natural. They claim that we have in us those principles from nature whence they flow. We respond that human nature did not contain these principles when it was first formed. They represent a later defilement and corruption, such as we see now. The philosophers take the visible effects and turn them into these existing principles.[1] But Christians understand them through the Word of God. Therefore, given that Scripture teaches that death entered through sin and that human beings as they were created would have lived forever [Rom. 5:12], let Pighius and those who follow him acknowledge just how pious and true their assertion is that death is a natural principle for a human being.

They add also that what cannot be avoided should not be counted as sin. This is patently false, given that none of us can perform the requirements of the Law or avoid all lapses against it as it is set forth. In weighing sins, we should not inquire whether anything is done through some causation or necessity, but only whether it violates or follows the Law of God. Wherefore, their arguments against us about necessity are inconsequential.

Lastly, they object that if sin derives from the first parents and flows to posterity, there can be no explanation why the sins of other parents should not be passed on to posterity. But if we grant this, they think the absurdity follows logically that those of us who are born last down the line will be in a terrible state, because we will have inherited, not just the sins of the first parents, but also all our ancestors.

---

1. He means that the philosophers, observing that humans suffer and die, reason from the effect to the principle to say that these principles are inherent to human nature.

41. The Schoolmen think that it is not possible that sins of the proximate parents pass over to the children. They seem to come to this conclusion for two reasons. The first of these is that the proximate parents only share with their children a nature and those other things which accompany nature as a matter of course. However, they do not share special properties and accidents, unless they by chance pertain to the body. For, often ancestral diseases, such as leprosy or gout, pass on to the children. But mental qualities are not derived from another, nor do they relate to procreation. A grammarian does not produce a grammarian, nor a musician a musician. Wherefore, since sins pertain to the mind, they say that these cannot be derived from their parents. A second reason is this: the first parents had original righteousness. This not only was situated in the mind, but also in the body and limbs. Therefore, by generating, they were able to transfer the lack of this righteousness to their children, since it adhered in the body and flesh. But the actual sins that followed thereafter, since they pertain to the mind, are not able to be spread to the children.

Nevertheless, Augustine in the *Enchiridion to Laurentius* 46 says that it is likely that the sins of the proximate parents are shared with the children. To prove it, he compared the two passages of Scripture with which we dealt. Seeing that God says that he will punish the sins of the parents in the children unto the third and fourth generation [Exod. 20:5], while in the other passage he says that the child will not bear the iniquity of the parent [Ezek. 18:20], he argues this: If the child does not bear the iniquity of the parent, but its own, and yet God punishes in the child the sin of the parent, it must be that the child has within itself that sin. Otherwise, these passages contradict. Therefore, sin is such in its own nature that it not only destroys the mind of a person, but also the body, and corrupts the flesh and its members. Therefore, Paul says to the Corinthians that our bodies are temples of the Holy Spirit. And he issues grave threats should a person destroy the temple of God [1 Cor. 6:19]. If, then, God punishes the sins of parents in their children, and the child does not bear another's iniquity but only its own, it follows that the infants of the impious, when they are afflicted, have something of their parents' corruption in themselves, so that the parents are punished in them. Mind you, we cannot call into question God's righteousness. If God by his most pure righteousness can deliver those who sin into a base inclination and punish sins with sins, why does he not also justly will that the corruption of sin not only destroy the mind, but also with its impurity contribute likewise to that of the body? From this they, who are begotten of sinners, draw such a nature from them as they find in them. And by this doctrine people are admonished to live holy lives, lest they pollute their own minds and bodies, and by the same deed infect also their own children.

42. If we are right about this, some will ask the difference between original sin and sin derived from the proximate parents. We respond that the spreading of original sin is perpetual, as the Holy Scriptures teach, but the continuation of other sins is not necessary. Sometimes no sin is transmitted to the children from the proximate parents, with the exception of original sin. It seems that God has predetermined a measure lest sin should go unchecked, and he has decided to temper this propagation of evil. Hezekiah, a most noble prince, had the very wicked king Ahaz

as his father; he, in turn, begat Ammon, a most wicked
child, who himself begat Manasses, who was even worse
[2 Kings 16:20; 20:21; 21:18]. Even if the beginnings of
sin are transferred to the children, sometimes God bestows
on them such grace, favor, and strength that they can overcome these things. But there is a way in which these do
not differ from original sin: for grace is conferred on the
godly so that they can have victory over it too. Also, when
God gives good children to evil parents, he declares the
power of his goodness, by which he checks the turpitude
and infection of the parents so that they do not pass down
to the children. In turn, when he brings it about that good
parents bear evil children, he shows his concern that the
godliness of children not be attributed to the merits of
the parents. They are not able to transfer grace to their
children by physical procreation, seeing that grace is an
altogether spiritual matter without any natural connection
with the flesh. Therefore, since goodness and godliness are
purely gifts from God, God does truly promise that he will
bless the posterity of pious people for a thousand generations. We must not understand this, however, as if some
merit is established in the ancestors. Mind you, God is induced by mercy alone to promise this, not by the merits of
people. Now, so that he might demonstrate his freedom,
sometimes he allows it to happen otherwise, teaching in
this way that godly parents are not so godly but that they
still have in them some depravity and corruption, which
they see engendered in their own children. From this we
can recognize the fallenness of our nature that accompa-
nies the godly all the way up to their death.

For establishing this doctrine still more, some adduce
from the Psalm the imprecation of the Church against the

wicked, "that they may be orphans, that no one will pity them, that they will beg for their food" [Psalm 109:9–10]. If the children of the wicked are guiltless, then this prayer is unjust. Wherefore, we are led to gather from these words that they share in the wickedness of their parents. For, seeing that they are small children, it cannot be by any other means but propagation. I know that there are some who want these words of David to be prophetic about the future, whereby the Holy Spirit foretells that these evils will befall them. It is undeniable that his words have in them the form and inclination of a prayer. But a prayer must be just, since otherwise it would not be a prayer.

43. As to their claim that this doctrine leads to an absurd consequence, that the last-born people will be the more miserable than all others, because they must bear the sins of Adam and all their forbearers, there are two responses. First, not all things that seem absurd to us are likewise absurd with God. Not to stray from the matter too far, Christ threatens the Jews that all the blood of the godly from Abel to Zechariah, the son of Berechiah, would be laid upon their charge. And who does not see that the condition of the sons of Israel who were carried off into captivity was more miserable than the very many generations of their ancestors who stained themselves with the same sins?

Second, we agree that it would be absurd if the sin of ancestors continually passed over to the children. Yet, seeing that we taught that it does not always happen, but the providence of God fixes an end and measure to this evil, and in that regard, he expressly spoke only of the third and fourth generation, there is no reason why it should seem absurd to anyone. The arguments of the Schoolmen against this spread of sin are very feeble. First, they teach that the properties of the mind are not communicated by the parents to the children, which experience teaches is false. Often, we see angry children born from angry parents, and sad from sad. Nor does it relate when they say that a grammarian is not born of a grammarian, a musician from a musician. Those are skills that are gained by learning the rules and going through training. They are not inclinations that are innate to people. And yet from experience we see it happen sometimes that the art in which a parent excelled, reemerges in children who exhibit a propensity for it, whether it be agriculture, soldiery, or liberal knowledge. Second, we are chiefly dealing with those inclinations here that are the starting-points and first principles of actions. In another argument, they say that sin in parents only corrupts the mind. This is not true, seeing that, as we taught above, their body is also stained. Therefore, it is no wonder if parents transfer such bodies to their children.

For this reason, so far as this goes, I gladly agree with Augustine that the concept of the spreading of sin through proximate parents is probable and consistent with Scriptures. Martin Bucer, a very learned man and no less godly, approved of this opinion that personal, individual sins are propagated from the parents to the children.[2] But, it must be noted that this is contingent, not necessary. God sometimes suspends the sins of the parents, and from his goodness does not allow human nature to be completely destroyed. Only he knows, however, when he will allow

---

2. Martin Bucer, *Common Places of Martin Bucer*, trans. and ed. D. F. Wright (Appleford: Sutton Courtenay, 1972), 135–36.

this sin to pass on or be checked. For us it is sufficient to consider these two facts: first, sin is spread from the parents unto the children; second, it is checked sometimes by God's goodness. This, though, cannot be said of original sin, for we are all born infected with it. This can be understood from Romans 5 by these words, "Through the disobedience...." See a similar passage: Genesis 8:21.

[CHAPTER 15:
DIGRESSION ON ROMANS 5:
SIN DEFINED]

I decided to add a section from chapter 5 of Paul's Letter to the Romans, on the words, "Just as through one man...."[1]

44. To understand the Apostle's words here clearly, we must examine three of his propositions: first, what he means by sin; second, who this one man is through whom sin entered into the world; third, how sin is spread.

First, the Apostle uses the term *sin* in a broad and general sense to indicate everything that opposes the Law and will of God. By this sin human beings withdrew from their natural composition and the archetype on which they were fashioned. God made them from the beginning in such a way that his image might shine forth in them. But, the opposite is true when we struggle against the divine Law. And this is the one and most true reason why human beings are not permitted to indulge themselves in any pleasure they choose. If a person does so, he comes near to the brute animals, not the likeness of God the Cre-

---

1. The final section is taken directly from Vermigli, *In Epistolam S. Pauli Apostoli ad Romanos*, 251–59; 501–8.

ator. Moreover, God wanted human beings to be overseers in the world, and therefore to be most like him. Indeed, sin understood in this broad sense not only encompasses original sin, that is, our depraved nature and the corrupted powers of our body and mind, but also all those evils following upon this. These include forbidden inclinations of the mind, sinful deliberations, evil pursuits, and corrupt habits. Therefore, by the single term *sin*, the Apostle includes both the root itself and all the fruits of it. We should not listen to those who prattle on that these are not sins. Given that the Holy Spirit terms them this, I see no reason why we should not also speak this way and acquiesce to this doctrine.

Second, the very etymology of the term sufficiently indicates that those initial mental impulses and our corrupt nature are sins. The Greek term ἁμαρτία comes from the verb ἁμαρτάνειν, a word that means "to stray from one's goal," however that happens. And since it is the guiding principle of our nature and all our actions to be conformed to God completely in all things, certainly when we are inclined to those things that God's Law forbids, and immediately rush headlong into them at the first prompting, it is indisputable that we must be said to sin, that is, to wander away from our goal and determined end. The Hebrew word has a similar sense. The word for sin in Hebrew is *Chataa*, drawn from the verb *Chata*, which you will find used in Judges 20 [v. 16] in the same way as I have said the Greek word ἁμαρτάνειν should be understood, that is, to wander from a goal. The passage in Judges talks about the seven hundred children of Benjamin who had so trained themselves in hurling stones from a sling that they could even hit a hair.

Additionally, experience itself teaches how grievous these sins are even in us regenerate. We are so impeded by them that we cannot fulfill the Law. However, we are bound to observe it on every point [Exod. 12:17]. We are commanded not to lust, a precept with which all of us agrees, yet witness how much we fight against ourselves by our proclivity to sin and first impulses to corrupt behavior. If the Fathers sometimes seem to write that the Law can be fulfilled by those regenerated in Christ, they are speaking about the beginnings of obedience and fulfillment of a sort that has much imperfection attached to it. They also proclaim that they are perfect and perform the Law of God who recognize their own defects, so that they may daily say among themselves, "Forgive us our debts," and acknowledge with Paul that they have much more progress to make. The same Fathers also confess that there is no one found, not even the most holy, who has absolutely loved all the virtues. As Jerome says, the one who excels others in one virtue often is deficient in another. And he cites Cicero, who said it is not easy to find one person who excels in the law or in eloquence. But, to find someone who is excellent in both is unheard of.

Therefore, to make the whole of God's blessing conferred on us through Christ be all the more eminently remarkable, the Apostle uses the term *sin* to mean more than just original sin. The term encompasses all kinds of vices that flow from original sin.

[CHAPTER 16:
DIGRESSION ON ROMANS 5:
HOW SIN ENTERS THE WORLD]

45. Now we must see by which *one man* Paul says sin of this sort entered into the world. He was the first Adam, who was, as it were, a kind of common lump or mass in which the whole human race was contained. Once this lump was polluted, people are not able to be born without being corrupted and depraved. And even though Eve transgressed before the man, the beginning of sinning is ascribed to Adam, since we trace lineage through men, not women. Ambrose, however, understood the phrase to mean *through one person* and to refer to Eve. But, since the adjective *one* is masculine in gender and can only indicate a male, it is not possible, except with great difficulty and force, for this phrase to refer to a female.

Others think that the generic word *person* refers to both Adam and Eve, so that this way of speaking does not differ much from that appearing in the second chapter of Genesis: "Male and female, he created them" [Gen. 2:27]. They are not bothered by the adjective *one*, because the Scripture testifies that Adam and Eve were one flesh [Gen. 2:24]. The first interpretation is simpler and easier, and so that is what I choose. We ought to remember, however, what Paul writes to Timothy that although both those first parents sinned, nevertheless in both there was not the same sort of transgression [1 Tim. 2:14]. He points out that Adam was not deceived. We can gather this from their response to God when he was reproving them. For, when the woman was asked why she did it, she accused the serpent, saying, "The serpent deceived me" [Gen. 3:13]. But Adam, when asked the same, did not say that he was deceived, but says, "The woman, whom you gave me, handed a fruit to me and I ate it" [Gen. 3:12]. One should not assume that this means that no error befell man when he transgressed. As it is clearly taught in the *Ethics*, in every kind of sin some error occurs.[1] Paul's point is this: man was not seduced by such a crass deception, but woman was. Paul is using this to support his command that a woman should keep silent in Church, since she has a disposition fit for being deceived. He confirmed it by the example of the first parents. She who pushed a man to sinning does not seem capable of rightly instructing him. And she who was capable of being seduced by the devil and deceived by the serpent is not suited to holding the rank of teacher in the Church.

Nevertheless, the book of Ecclesiastes says that sin began with the woman [Eccl. 25:33]. We cannot refute this if we consider the story as it unfolds in Genesis. But Paul, as we just now said, sticks to the usual custom of Scripture when he ascribes propagation to men, not women. In the

---

1. Aristotle, *Nicomachean Ethics* 3.1.

present passage of Romans his aim was not to indicate which sinned first, Adam or Eve, but to show the root from which sin was spread in the world. And so is that likewise resolved which may be objected out of the book of Wisdom, that by the envy of the devil, sin entered the world [2:24]. John also writes that the devil sinned from the beginning [1 John 3:8]. In Paul's passage the issue is not the imitation of another's sin or the persuading to sin. Otherwise, it is true that the first example of sin came from the devil. He also was the persuader to and author of transgressions. But the Apostle's aim in the Romans passage is to teach the source from which original sin was passed by propagation to the human race. The Apostle wants to be able to prove by the antithesis between Christ and the first Adam, that the Lord did not restore us or make us righteous only by setting an example before us to imitate, or by showing himself to be a faithful moral guide, but by changing us completely and by restoring us through Spirit and grace. For this reason, Augustine seems to have expressed correctly the trouble brought on by Adam when he says that he laid waste to the human race. He uses this word to indicate that he infected all of us with a kind of contagion.

46. Against this opinion the Pelagians usually argue the following: That which does not exist cannot cause harm. Moreover, original sin, if there is any, is wiped away by faith in Christ and baptism, and no longer exists. Therefore, it cannot harm the children that are baptized.[2]

But their premise that original sin is wiped out of believers and the baptized is not completely true, seeing

---

2. That is, the parents cannot propagate what was removed from them.

that in the case of any sin we must consider two things: the action or depraved affection, which is like the material, and the offence or obligation to the punishment, which they call guilt. But original sin differs from those sins that are called *actual,* because in them the material does not persist or endure. When someone commits adultery or speaks a blasphemy, those actions, once completed, immediately cease to be, nor do they exist any longer. Only the offense against God and guilt before him remains. Wherefore, since by faith and repentance the obligation to punishment and the offense against God is remitted, we easily concede that the whole sin is wiped away. But in the case of original sin there is another arrangement, because its material does not pass away. Each one of us has a sense in ourselves that a corrupt nature remains, since we keep rushing headlong into sin. Moreover, we are incompetent when it comes to divine things, both in mind and body, though these are sins that are not imputed to the faithful. Our guilt and offense against God are forgiven in baptism by faith in Christ, though the material of sin still remains. Although in godly people it is weakened and broken, still we will not attain the perfect wiping away of it until we die. And since the regenerate procreate, and this, not wherein they are renewed, but by nature and flesh, it comes about that their children are born bound by original sin. A sinful and corrupt nature is poured forth into them such as is in the parents, while on the other hand forgiveness or imputation, which are received by faith, cannot be spread to them.

To explain this, Augustine uses a twofold simile: the kernels of grain, which are sown stripped of their leaves, chaff, straw, and ears are born again with all those things.

This happens because the purging takes place, not by nature, but by human ingenuity and industry. And since the new stalks spring, not from the initial ingenuity and industry, but from nature, it must be that things coming into being follow, not the mode of human industry, but that of nature itself. The second simile concerns a circumcised man, who nevertheless procreates a son with a foreskin. Circumcision was not in the father by nature but applied by force from the outside. Since the children are not procreated by that external force but by the internal force of nature, they follow the order of nature when coming into being. We produce children such as we ourselves are. Wherefore, seeing that we have in us an original contagion, they cannot lack it. Moreover, we are not able to communicate the remission and forgiveness of that sin to our children. We must hope for that from God alone. We see the very same thing in the case of the sciences and virtues: although they are in the parents, nevertheless, they are not passed on to the offspring.

From these examples we can see sufficiently wherein the Pelagians are deceived. Nor can anyone rightly cast aspersions on us in this regard, as if we disparage faith or baptism. For, we concede wholeheartedly that baptism seals in us the remission of guilt and offense, grace, the Spirit, the ingrafting into Christ, and the right to eternal life. But, it does not follow that by it our natural corruption or the kindling of sin is abolished. In this regard Paul says rightly, "We are saved by hope" [Rom. 8:14]. It is a wonder how the Pelagians deny that there is original sin in infants, since every day we see that they die. Scripture clearly teaches that "the wages of sin is death, and the sting of death is sin" [Rom. 6:23]. Therefore, you must necessarily remove the possibility of death from whomever you remove sin. Scripture testifies that these are in a cause and effect relationship. The one exception is Christ, who, although he did not know our sin, died for our sake. But death in him did not hold sway. He willingly endured it for our salvation. But to affirm that some die without sin is to join together things that are repugnant and contrary. Besides this passage, there are many others that can prove that infants do not lack sin. David says, "Behold I was conceived in iniquities, and in sins my mother conceived me" [Psalm 51:7]. And Paul in Ephesians calls us by nature children of wrath [Eph. 3:3]. And in Genesis it is written, "The heart of a person from infancy is prone to evil" [Gen. 8:21]. Other passages besides those already cited support this doctrine.

[CHAPTER 17:
DIGRESSION ON ROMANS 5:
HOW SIN IS PROPAGATED]

47. I have explained what the Apostle means by sin, and identified through which one man it entered into the world; it remains for us to see how it was propagated. The matter is obscure and very difficult, so I have decided to spend less time on it. Because the Word of God teaches lucidly that original sin exists and is transmitted to posterity, although we do not understand the mode whereby it is spread, we must yield to the truth. We should not vex ourselves too much in dispute about the mode, however, since it is difficult to comprehend and causes us no trouble if we do not know it. It will not hurt, however, to rehearse those modes I have observed in the ecclesiastical writers.

I find four opinions among them. The first opinion is that we receive from our parents our souls along with our bodies, so that, just as God fashions the body through human seed, so he creates the soul from the same. Augustine refers to this opinion in *Genesis ad literam* 10 and in many other places, nor does he ever express his disapproval of it, as far as I recall. Rather, he says that through this opinion the knot concerning original sin can be loosened. Tertullian and many ancient writers favored this opinion. I judge their arguments probable but not necessary. That which they adduce from Genesis 46 [v. 26] about the sixty-six souls produced from the loins of Jacob can be explained suitably as a synecdoche, so that by the soul, which is the superior part of a person, the body is meant, which no one doubts is produced from the seed of the parents. By soul we can also understand the crasser parts of the soul, such as the vegetative parts and the feeling part, which no one doubts are procreated from seed. Moreover, Christ testifies in the Gospel that sometimes Scriptures uses soul in this sense when he says, "The one who loses his soul for my sake will find it" [Mark 16:25].

The second means, as Augustine writes in book ten on Genesis, is this: In the creation of the woman we do not read that God breathed into her a living soul. From this they gather that she not only took her body from Adam, but also her soul. Augustine considers this a weak rationale. One can retort that it had already been said that God breathed into Adam, and therefore there was no need for repetition. If a new mode of procreation had been introduced, Scripture would not have passed over it in silence. Because Scripture makes no mention of a new mode, we must use that which it expressed before, especially since we see that Adam said about his own wife, "This now is bone of my bones, and flesh of my flesh" [Gen. 2:14]. He did not add that she was "soul of my soul," which would have been an especially attractive addition and would have served nicely to express the union of marriage. But

Augustine admits that this does not resolve the question. If we establish that souls are created each and every day, and are created in such a way that there is no pre-existing *seminal structure* (as Augustine himself terms it) in the bodies, then God will not seem to have completely ceased his labor on the seventh day, since he continues daily to create souls from nothing.[1] But perhaps we can respond to this argument that it is sufficient in the body passed down from the parents if the qualities and conditions are found that make it able to receive a rational soul, and that this is the seminal structure.

48. Whatever we are to make of these arguments and answers, we can say for sure that Augustine is inclined to think that at least the soul of Christ did not issue forth from the blessed virgin through propagation. He says that others before him held the same opinion and held that it could be proven by the statement in Hebrews, "The priesthood of Christ surpassed the priesthood of Aaron, because Christ is a priest according to the order of Melchizedek" [Heb. 7:3]. Moreover, the priesthood of Melchizedek was greater than that of Aaron, because Levi gave tithes to Melchizedek. The one who was made to pay tithes to Melchizedek was in the loins of Abraham. But Christ too should have been no less in the loins of Abraham than was Levi, had he received his soul and body from him. And so, in this regard, they should have had equal dignity

---

1. By *seminal structure* Augustine refers to the seeds necessary for the existence of everything. God created these during the original creation, according to this argument, and from them all things that come into being derive, relieving God of the need to create new things from nothing.

to each other, given that they were made to pay tithes to Melchizedek.

At this point, those who favor these ideas could respond that there is some other difference between Christ and Levi, because, although both were in the loins of Abraham, body and soul, nevertheless they do not derive their nature from him in the same manner. Christ was born of the virgin Mary by intervention of the Holy Spirit, but Levi was begotten and born in the common way whereby other people are propagated. Therefore, Augustine dismisses this passage as a proof and adduces another out of the Book of Wisdom [8:19], where, as he understands it, we are to imagine Christ speaking: "I have obtained a good soul by lot."[2] He thinks that this phrase cannot stand if the soul of Christ was derived through propagation by the law of nature through forefathers, unless we are willing to affirm that nature works by chance. And he thinks that this term *lot* is applied to the soul of Christ so that we can understand that those ornaments, with which his soul is bountifully supplied, were not bestowed because of any pre-existing merits, but through the pure mercy of God; and that this was the ultimate ornament of Christ, to be joined to the same hypostasis and person with the Word of God. But since he did not take this testimony from one of the canonical books, it has little strength to it.

Lastly, he leaves the question of the transmitting of souls up in the air, as if either side is probable. And those who oppose it cite Psalm 33 [v. 15]: "Who fashioned individually their hearts." He says that this is also a weak proof

---

2. Augustine, *De peccatorum meritis et remissione* 1.38 (*On the Merits*, NPNF, 5:29).

passage, since those who assert that souls are transmitted likewise agree that God is the Creator, though they counter that he works through the means of propagation. We read in the book of Genesis that the birds were not created out of nothing, but they sprang forth from the waters by the command of God. And each one of us is said to dissolve back into the dust of the earth whence we came, though we do not derive directly from the earth, but from the bodies of our parents.

49. This opinion cannot be refuted and overturned by the Scriptures, although I know it is the received opinion of the Church that souls in creating are infused, and in infusing are created. Nor have I recounted these things because I want at all to alter this doctrine, but only so that it can be understood what mode of the propagation of original sin seemed most easy to some ecclesiastical writers. Certainly, the Schoolmen, when they refute this opinion, use only natural reasons. They say that the soul, rational by nature, cannot be cut up, seeing that it is completely spiritual and indivisible, though if it is derived from the parents it would be divisible. And since in their view it is intelligent and too dignified to be drawn from what matter has to offer, they argue that it must come to being through creation, not generation.

Augustine mentions another way that sin could be propagated in his book *On Marriage and Concupiscence*, and in many other places, where he debates the Pelagians about this kind of sin.[3] Sin flows into the offspring, he says, through that pleasure that the parents take from in-

3. Augustine, *De nuptiis et concupiscentia* 1.27 (*On Marriage and Concupiscence*, NPNF, 5:274–75).

tercourse. But, this manner of spreading relies on a suspect foundation, and one that is in my judgment not true. The pleasure which is taken from procreation is not of its own nature evil, unless it contains sinful desire. If the action itself has sin attached to it out of necessity, then the Holy Spirit would not exhort any one to it. But he does, when he encourages marriage, and when through Paul he advises spouses to exchange mutual feelings of love to one another. But if we agree and grant that sexual relations contain a degree of sin, it would follow that only this kind of lust flows down into the offspring. But the stain of original sin lies not only in our sexual lusts, but in lusts of other kinds, such as the lust of wealth, prestige, and revenge, as well as in the whole corruption of our nature.

The third explanation of the propagation of sin is that God creates the soul with a fault of this sort, or defect, because it will be the soul of a person already damned and constituted under the curse. God creates the sort of soul, they say, that is required for such a person, just as we see that for the body of a dog he gives a canine's animating spirit, and an ass's animating spirit to the body of an ass. But this opinion seems the hardest, to say that God contaminates a soul with sin that does not yet relate to Adam, especially since they cannot say that this kind of sin is the punishment of another's sin that preceded it. Therefore, this fantasy is usually rejected, lest we seem to make God directly the author of sin.

A fourth explanation is favored by a majority and seems most likely true. It says that the soul is not created with sin, but contracts it immediately when it makes contact with the body that is descended from Adam. For, seeing that it lacks the grace and the strength with which the soul of the first human was endowed, and has obtained a body subject to the curse, and has instruments inadequate and unsuited to spiritual works, therefore, when it should rule over the body, it is burdened and weighed down by it, and drawn to the desires that are appropriate to the body. It is hampered on both sides, both by the impurity of the body and by its own weakness, bereft, as it is, of those powers whereby it could surpass nature. From these two heads stems the corruption and depravity of the whole nature.

I have said as much as I thought is sufficient for this present purpose, how the Apostle understands the word *sin*, through whom it is said to have flowed into the human race, and what the theologians have traditionally taught about its mode of transmission.

50. But Augustine argues strongly against the errors of the Pelagians in his book *On the Merits*, where he shows that the body of the first man was not of necessity subject to death, though he was mortal, because if he did sin, he must die.[4] This does not mean that he thinks it is right to say, "This one is mortal; therefore, he will surely die." We might concede that our flesh can be wounded, and yet it is possible that it does not receive a wound; likewise, the body of human beings is, one might say, capable of sickness, yet we see that sometimes people die before they become sick. Therefore, he says that the state of Adam's body was such that, although it could die, this is true only if sin intervened, otherwise he would have been preserved by God, just as the clothes and the sandals of the Hebrews

---

4. Augustine, *De peccatorum meritis et remissione* 2.35 (*On the Merits*, NPNF, 5:58).

in the desert, by God's power, were not worn out or ru-
ined for forty years, as we read in Deuteronomy 19. And
he thinks that, in reference to their condition, Enoch and
Elisha now are in that state that Adam's body was, because
they were kept from death. And he thinks that either they
are sustained without food or they enjoy nourishment pre-
pared for them by God. Indeed, the first man had food
whereby he was nourished and was eating other fruits to
keep from wasting away. But he was eating from the tree
of life as a remedy for old age. This tree provided a replen-
ishment of what was used up that possessed no less benefit
and wholeness than that which was lost. Moreover, we see
that the same does not happen in us, and we struggle with
old age and finally death takes hold of us.

In Adam, therefore, there was a condition of mortality, but one which was to be absorbed by the kindness of
God when he was translated at the right time to the utmost felicity.[5] Starting from this premise, Augustine determined that we are not able to comprehend the greatness of
Christ's blessing, since he restored to us more than Adam
took away. Through Christ, not only was life restored to
us and death repelled, but mortality was also removed in
the resurrection. We will not be able to die, as Paul teaches
when he writes that this mortal self will put on immortality [1 Cor. 15:54]. He seems to be teaching this same
idea to the Romans when he says, "But if Christ dwells in
us, the body is dead because of sin" [8:10]. Here he is not
saying that our body by sin is mortal, but dead, that is, in
the grip of death. Then he adds, "His Spirit which raised

---

5. That is, if he had not sinned. See Augustine, *De peccatorum meritis
et remissione* 1.2 (*On the Merits*, NPNF, 5:15).

Christ from the dead will give life to your mortal bodies"
[v. 11]. He says this concerning the resurrection, when
our bodies, which he called mortal, not dead, must be
brought to life, so that you may understand that, not only
is death to be removed from them, but also they will be no
longer mortal. As to what the Pelagians think, that death
should be taken allegorically for the fall of souls, it cannot
be allowed, since in Romans 5 it is written, "Through one
man sin entered into the world and through sin death" [v.
11]. But if the death introduced by Adam was only that
of souls, why did Paul express his point twofold, not only
saying *sin*, but also adding *death*? Besides, the testimony of
Genesis most plainly refutes them, where the punishment
of man is described thus: "Earth you are, and into earth
you shall return" [Gen. 3:19]. Whether they want to or
not, they are forced to conclude that this has to do with
the death of the body, unless they dare to say that our souls
are fashioned from the earth and also are to be dissolved
into the earth. And their point of contention, namely, that
we have a body fused by nature out of opposites, is of little
importance, since its preservation depends, not on nature,
but on God, as Scripture shows happened in the case of
the clothes and the shoes of the Hebrews [Deut. 19:5].

51. What he means when he uses the word *death* can
best be understood from its antithesis, *life*. This life is of
two sorts: one, whereby we are moved to spiritual, divine,
and celestial good things, only happens if we are united
with God. Unless we are led by the spirit, we are not able
to strive for those things which surpass our nature. The
other is a life whereby we are moved to pursue those good
things that have to do with preserving our nature and
maintaining our corporeal state.

Each of these two lives did death, which has been imposed because of sin, take away. Death, you see, is nothing other than the deprivation of life. As soon as man sinned, he was turned away from God. Man lost his grace and was stripped of his favor such that he was not able to aspire again to eternal joy. Sin also removed the bodily life, for immediately after sin entered, the beginnings of death and its accomplices invaded man, among which are hunger, thirst, disease, physical imbalances, and organ failure, and the slow, daily decline. All these lead a person to death. And Chrysostom, dealing extensively with this matter in his reflections on Genesis, says that man and woman were dead immediately upon sinning.[6] The Lord pronounced the sentence of death against them on the spot. And just as those who have received a capital sentence for a time linger alive in prison, yet still are reckoned for dead, so the first parents, though from the kindness of God continued to live for a time, nevertheless, in reality, were dead immediately after their sentences were pronounced. Ambrose says that they were suddenly overcome by death because afterwards they had no day, hour, or moment in which they were not subject to it.[7] Nor are there any mortals who can promise themselves that they will live one hour.

From these things, it is apparent that both deaths were brought on by sin. For this reason, we must be on guard not to agree with those who often say that death is natural to man, as if it is some rest interrupting life's activ-

---

6. Chrysostom, *Homilia in Genesim* 17.42 (*Homilies on Genesis 1–17*, 245).

7. Perhaps a reference to *De paradiso* 43 (*On Paradise*, 321).

ity. Opinions of this sort must be left to the unsaved races. All the pious believe that in dying we are experiencing God's wrath. Therefore, by its very nature death inflicts grief and dread. Christ himself states this very thing while praying in the garden, as do many other holy people.

But if some find it sweet and desirable to die and to be freed from life, they have other reasons unrelated to the nature of death. And Paul says to the Corinthians that death is the sting of sin [1 Cor. 15:56]. For, death could otherwise have no power over us unless it consumes us through sin. Therefore, those who proclaim that original sin is only some weakness that cannot bring damnation on a person do not understand the nature of sin nor this teaching of the Apostle that we have before us.

Furthermore, if death flows from sin, all sins by their own nature must be called mortal. The fact that God does not impute some sins to us does not stem from the lightness of sins, but from his mercy. There can be no sin light enough not to merit destruction, unless the mercy of God interposes itself. Even so, we cannot agree with the Stoics when they say that all sins are equal, since we know that Paul describes some of our sins as being so grave that they exclude people from the kingdom of Heaven.

On barrenness, hunger, thirst, floods, plague, and the causes of such calamities, see 1 Kings 8:37 and Genesis 26:7.

[CHAPTER 18:
DIGRESSION ON ROMANS 5:
CREATURES AND THE FALL]

52. All creatures, however, await our revelation, because in the meantime every creature is subject to vanity. This passage of Paul is difficult, but I think its sense is sufficiently clear, namely, that every creature lives in a grievous state and is worn down by vexing woes until our full redemption. Because of us, the earth is subject to a curse, producing thorns and thistles, and to nourish us requires a cycle of bloom and decay. It is compelled to endure damage and devastation for our sins. The air is full of disease, vacillating between extremes of heat and cold, sometimes darkened with clouds and rains. Living creatures of all kinds are propagated and die for our benefit. The celestial bodies are constantly prodded; they die, they arise, they suffer eclipses. The moon waxes and wanes. In the death of Christ, the light of the sun was blocked; and when he comes against to judge, as the evangelists tell, the powers of the heavens will be in distress.

Furthermore, all creation is compelled to serve the impious and be subject to their abuses. Hosea teaches this in the second chapter, saying that the Israelites were ascribing the blessings of this world, in which they were abounding, not to the true God, as was right, but to Baal. They were giving thanks to him and invoking only him. Therefore, God said in his anger, "I will take away grain, my wine, my oil; and I will free my wool and my flax, lest they cover your shame" [Hosea 2:9]. By these words the prophet shows that when created things are taken away from the ungodly, they are set free and are not forced to be enslaved to them any longer.

Augustine in book 83 of *Quaestions*, question 67, interprets Paul's passage differently. By the phrase *every creature* he understands human beings, a sense we also find in the Gospel. Christ says this: "Proclaim the Gospel to every creature" (Mark 16:15). Therefore, in his view the application of the phrase to human beings is certainly fitting because mankind is a kind of microcosm of everything. However, he does admit that the passage could be interpreted in other ways. But he cautions against the foolish idea that the sun, moon, stars, and heavenly angels actually groan, as some are not ashamed to imagine. He agrees that the holy angels serve us at God's bidding, but since they are blessed and see the face of the Father, it cannot be that they groan and ache because of us, lest by chance they seem to be in a worse state than Lazarus was in the bosom of Abraham. Add to this the fact that Paul says that every creature is subject to vanity, and not only groans and aches, but also must be freed from corrupt servitude. None of this can be applied to the nature of angels. But, Augustine says, we must not rashly assert anything. It is enough that we watch out for the absurd and foolish opinions of heretics, who have uttered many false things about the moaning and groaning of creatures. He is alluding to the Manicheans, among others.

53. In speaking about Augustine's opinion that by the phrase *every creature* we should understand *men*, I note that all mankind should be divided into two parts: some men are pious, some impious. Then we must ask which of these with great desire await the revelation or manifestation of the sons of God. I think this does not apply to the impious. They do not consider what will happen in the age to come to be of any importance. Therefore, only the pious remain, and as such, incontrovertibly, we should call them sons of God. It follows, then, that they alone are sons of God who await the revelation of the sons of God. Thus, the same will be those who desire and who are desired. Yet, it seems that this did not escape Augustine's notice, for he says that the sons of God, seeing that now they are burdened by manifold troubles, desire a better state which they hope at some point will be revealed. True, it often happens that those who are in a troublesome and difficult situation desire strongly to be granted eventually a more peaceful lot. But, if we consider those things which soon Paul adds, "not only those, but also we who have the first fruits of the Spirit..." we will see that pious people are being put in a distinct position, and that those endowed with the Spirit of God are separated from the host of other creatures. This is what the phrase *not only* implies.

However, I know there are some who, by those who are said to have the first fruits of the Spirit, do not understand all Christians universally, but only those who at that point in time were abounding with a great supply of the Spirit, such as were the Apostles, that is, Paul himself, and a few others endowed with the apostolic spirit. It is as if it were being said, "The revelation of the glory of the sons of God is expected not only by all the pious, but also by us endowed with the abundant spirit of Christ," thereby bolstering and amplifying the argument by the judgment of the best and wisest men.

But the Apostle does not seem to use that distinction in the present passage. Previously, he proclaimed universally that we who are of Christ have his Spirit dwelling in us. Nor does he mean to draw a distinction between the common Christian and the Apostles by mentioning the first fruits of the Spirit. Instead, he called the first fruits of the Spirit *this Spirit that we now have*, because in the future life we will have the full fruits of him and an abundant harvest. And Ambrose, in interpreting this passage, adds immediately, "After speaking about creatures as a whole, he now speaks about men themselves."

The arguments also, whereby Augustine was led to abandon the common interpretation of the passage, are not weighty and solid enough to attribute much to them. When Paul has inanimate things desire our salvation, and for its sake to groan and be vexed, he means it as a personification. To think otherwise is to play the fool with the heretics and believe absurd things about the sun, moon, and stars.

Here we are in doubt about two figures: Augustine understood every creature to signify mankind; but we think it is just a personification. The controversy here is which figure should be applied. I think we should take the one that agrees more with the words of the Apostle and makes the argument weightier and more forceful. Since our interpretation does both, I think it should be applied. First, the Apostle added, as we noted, "Not only those, but also we who have the first fruits of the Spirit...." These words sufficiently indicate that he referred previously to the other creatures, and not people. Second, this explanation serves well to augment our redemption, which we await, if we understand that it is expected by every kind of creature.

54. This exposition of Paul's passage runs into a difficulty when we come to the matter of angels. They would seem to me to be in a miserable state if for our sake they either groan or feel the pangs of distress. We should think that they are blessed and holy.

Yet, their happiness does not make it so that they are completely stripped of every kind of emotion. Peter in his first epistle in the first chapter says that they "long to look upon the promises of the prophets that pertain to the Gospel" [v. 12]. We reject the translation, "upon whom they desire to look," and prefer, "upon which they desire to look." In other words, they are held by the desire of seeing these promises fulfilled. In Zechariah, we read that they, among the myrtle trees, like a troop of horsemen, prayed with great emotion for the holy city to be built again [Zech. 1:12]. I pass over the fact that we read in the Gospel they are said to experience great joy when they see sinners turned to repentance [Luke 15:10]. For this reason, we are compelled to argue just the opposite, that they feel anxious over the rebellion and stubbornness of the impious. No one doubts that the souls of godly people who have already died are endowed with the utmost happiness. Even so, in the Apocalypse they shout and pray for God to avenge the blood which has been shed; and with great emotion they clamor for the cloak of their body, which is now corrupted, to be restored to them at some point [6:10].

Thus, we must attribute a happiness both to the angels and blessed souls that does not exclude those kinds of emotions that Scripture indicates they possess. This should seem less surprising given that we read in Scriptures that God himself, the font and source of all happiness, feels regret, changes his mind, and experiences many other emotions which do not seem to fit with his divine nature. It is not our inclination to explain how we should understand these things, nor is it needed here. It will be sufficient to say briefly that the angels can experience such emotions, as Paul mentions in this passage. But even if we cannot understand how it does not hinder happiness, there is no reason for denying that it can happen. It will only be clear to us when we achieve that same happiness. Meanwhile, let us put our trust in the Sacred Scriptures, which bear witness that the holy angels are troubled by emotions of this sort.

55. But how do we understand that they are subject to vanity? The answer is easy: not according to the substance of their nature, as they say, but so far as relates to those works that God decreed they should accomplish. They preside over states, kingdoms, and provinces, as Daniel so eloquently writes [10:13]. Yes, they are present for every individual. For, as Christ says, "Their angels will always behold the face of my father" [Mark 18:10]. And the disciples in Acts of the Apostles when someone was knocking at the door, "It is his angel" [Acts 12:15]. Some interpret this to mean this is Peter's messenger. And in Genesis 48 [v. 16]: "His angel delivered me from evil." These prove

that angels, by the command of God, do service even to private individuals.

However, if we wish to ask to what end the angels govern kings, provinces, cities, and individuals, and what they mean by such great care and diligence, we will find nothing other than that they are busy making sure that all men obey God their King, and that they acknowledge and worship him, revering him as their own God. Because the angels fail in this and many men give themselves over to superstition and idolatry, leaving behind the true worship of God, and defile themselves with many shameful acts, we can say that the efforts of the angels fall short of their own purpose, at least their secondary purpose, and thus they are in a sense subject to vanity. This will cease to be when they are discharged from their oversights.

But now it must be seen how the angels are freed at that time from the slavery of corruption. We can answer this from their nature or, as they say, their substance. Their nature or, as some term it, substance is incorruptible and immortal, nevertheless they involve themselves continuously with fallen things and mortals. These things they constantly repair and sustain, or according to divine precept, ensure that they are taken away and destroyed. Second, the gift of Christ pertains likewise to the angels, as Paul teaches in the letters to the Ephesians and Colossians. In Ephesians 1 [v. 10] he says, "According to the good pleasure which he purposed in himself, even to the dispensation of the fulness of times, to make all things anew through Christ, both which are in heaven and which are in earth." And in Colossians 1 [v. 20]: "It has well pleased the Father that in him should dwell all fulness, and by him to reconcile all things to himself; and to set at peace through the blood of his cross both the things in heaven and the things in earth." Chrysostom, interpreting this, says that without Christ the angels were hostile to us, so that these two natures, that of angels and of human beings, were severed and alienated from each other. For, the heavenly spirits could not but hate the enemies of their God. But, since Christ interposed himself, now human beings have been brought back into the fold so that they have the same head with the angels, and they have been made members of the same body with him. Therefore, Christ is rightly said to be the one through whom our reunion[1] is effected.

Also, it is possible that the angels receive other benefits through the death of Christ that the Scriptures have not revealed to us and that we have no way of finding out. Therefore, we say that with great weight and vehemence Paul applies emotions and sense to all creatures, as if they feel grieved that they are so exposed to the abuses of ungodly people. The confusion of things in the present state is obvious. The pious suffer and everywhere are treated badly. Meanwhile, the ungodly live in affluence and have their way. In this state of upheaval, the godly must be courageous and patiently await the overturning of the situation.

Epicureans and atheists, when they see all things plunged into such confusion, straightaway rationalize that God is not concerned with mortals, seeing that he is moved neither by favor nor hatred, and does neither ill or good to anyone. The godly in contrast assure themselves that the future will be of a different sort, since God conducts and

---

1. Literally, our recapitulation, that is, the regathering of men and angels under one head.

governs all things by his providence. They believe too that
the world must be corrected and made better, according
as it was created for God's glory, and must be transformed
into that form whereby God may more and more be mag-
nified. And from this arises an incredible consolation, that
when we see all the creatures of God subject to so many
troubles, we by their example also find strength to endure.
Given that the whole world is vexed by so many calamities, it is fitting that we also calmly tolerate the afflictions
that befall us.

56. In addition, we can enumerate four reasons why
we think that the creatures grieve and suffer.

The first is that they are fatigued by the endless toil
required to serve our daily needs. Hence, frequently they
pay the price with us for our repeated and grave sinning, a
fact made obvious in the case of the flood, in Sodom, and
in the plagues of Egypt. Additionally, there exists a kind of
sympathy among all creatures and mankind, whereby in
adversity they groan and suffer with human beings. Finally, they experience great harm from being forced to serve
human beings who are both impure and wicked. Hosea
the prophet saw this, as we showed above, when he was
speaking on behalf of God: "I will carry off my wheat, my
wine, my oil, and I will release my wool and flax, lest they
work your filthiness" [Hosea 2:8].

Ambrose makes my case in several places. In the *Epistle to Horontianus*,[2] while dealing with this passage of Paul,
he shows by induction that "every creature groans and
awaits the revealing of the sons of God." He begins with
the soul, which he says cannot help but be afflicted and

---

2. This entire section refers to Ambrose, *Epistles* 34.

made sad, since it sees itself encased in the body as if in a kind of quagmire. This is so, not because it wants it this way, but because of him who subjected it. It was God's plan to join the soul with the body so that from the association it might return some fruits one day. Paul says in 2 Corinthians that "we will all be set before the tribunal of Christ, so that each one give account of those things done through the body, whether good or evil" [5:10]. He also says in the same epistle, "We groan while in this earthly dwelling; not because we wish to be cleaned of it, but rather to be covered over with a garment" [2 Cor. 5:4]. And Ambrose cites this from the Psalms: "Man is made like to vanity" [Psalm 144:4], and that man is "altogether vanity" [Psalm 39:6]. To these I think this must also be added: we should keep in mind that this burden of the body and these troubles, which David complains about while thinking about his situation, do not stem from God's creation, but instead crept in because of sin. Otherwise, the body was given to the mind, not as a tomb, as some imagine, but as the most suitable instrument for accomplishing the most remarkable and exceptional deeds.

Ambrose continues, reasoning through induction that the sun, moon, and other stars are fatigued by their own course, and that the creatures below are vexed for our sake.[3] He further says that they do so, not with resentment, since they understand that the very son of God assumed the form of a servant on our behalf and by his death secured our life and salvation. Second, he says, they console themselves with the knowledge that some day they will be set free and an end will be placed on their distress.

---

3. Ambrose, *Epistle* 34.7.

If I am to pass judgment on these statements, first, I really doubt whether the sun, moon, and other stars labor and feel vexed as a result of their revolutions. Furthermore, I think Ambrose is speaking figuratively when he says that all creatures bear their troubles with a calm mind because they know that Christ the son of God bore the shame and death of the cross for our salvation. He is likewise speaking figuratively when he says that they console themselves with the knowledge that their own labors at some point will come to an end and that they themselves will be repaired.

Lastly, he makes the statement that the angels do not enjoy punishing evil people, because they are touched with mercy and prefer to adorn them with benefits rather than afflict them with punishments.[4] This is reinforced, he says, when Christ in Luke says that the angels strongly rejoice when one person repents of sin [Luke 15:10]. Also, in expounding upon this passage, Ambrose says that the angst of the creatures will endure until the number of the saved is fulfilled. And he interprets *to be subject to vanity* as referring to their mortal and transitory nature. Therefore, he considers vanity in this passage to refer to the mortality whereby the whole creation labors, thus compelled to struggle constantly with it, as Solomon justly said: "Vanity of vanities, all is vanity" [Eccl. 1:12].

57. The commentaries which are ascribed to Jerome do not seem to differ much from the opinion of Augustine, except that they understand by *every creature* the entirety of those who exist now back all the way to Adam. The commentaries hold that this whole crowd of saints,

---

4. Ambrose, *Epistle* 34.10.

together with the first man, anxiously awaits the revelation of the sons of God, so that they themselves with us, as Hebrews teaches, might be perfected [Heb. 11:40]. Origen makes mention of certain things concerning the mind, which is the highest part of our soul.[5] He says it groans and anxiously grieves that it is compelled to humble itself to serve the many and varied requirements of the body. But Chrysostom clearly supports our point of view, asserting that Paul is personifying the creation. This trope is very familiar from the Scriptures. The prophets and the Psalms command the waters and the woods sometimes to clap their hands [Psalm 47:1]. Sometimes they have the mountains dancing and the hills jumping for joy. This is not because they attach movement and sensation to inanimate objects, but to signify that the good thing which they commend is so great that it ought to pertain also to the creatures who are without sense and feeling. Sometimes the prophets have the woods, the vines, the earth, and the other elements howling and shouting, as well as the roofs of houses and temples shouting, in order to stress more vehemently the evil that they are describing [Isaiah 24:4]. It should not be a surprise if Paul imitates these phrases of the prophets, seeing that the same Spirit of God was in each.

58. It is not difficult to demonstrate how our misfortunes redound also to the creatures. For, when judgment was passed on mankind that it be cursed, the earth was also condemned as cursed, so that is forced to produce thorns and thistles [Gen. 3:17]. And how it has been ren-

---

5. This comes from his *Commentary on the Epistle to the Romans* 7.4.9, pp. 69–71.

dered barren and squalid because of sin, both Scripture
everywhere teaches us, as does experience, if we are paying attention. Isaiah says in chapter 24 [v. 23], "The sun
is confounded and the moon blushes." And in reference
to the destruction of Babylon the same prophet writes,
"The moon and the stars will not give light; the sun will
be shrouded in darkness" [Isaiah 13:10]. Concerning the
heavens, David proclaims, "From the beginning the heavens are the works of your hands; they will perish, yet you
remain; you will change them as a garment, and they will
be changed" [Psalm 102:26]. Moses says in the Law, "I will
give a heaven of bronze, an earth of iron" [Deut. 28:23].
We know this was done in the time of Elijah, when the sky
was so shut up that for the span of three and a half years it
did not provide rain [2 Kings 17:1; Lam. 5:17]. This is the
sense behind that enigmatic prophesy of Hosea [2:21]: "I
will hear the heavens speaking, and the heavens will hear
the earth, and the earth will hear the grain, the wine, and
oil, and they will hear Israel."

Finally, in what sense every creature serves godly people, the Scriptures indicate everywhere. The sea opened
a path for the Israelites; the rock poured forth water; the
sky provided the cloud and manna; the sun stood still for
Joshua and went back for Hezekiah [Exod. 14:21; 16:13;
17:6; Josh. 10:13; Isaiah 38:8]. We can see these things en-
capsulated in the life of Christ, where they are wondrously
and miraculously repeated. At his birth, the heavens rejoice
and shine at night; the angels stand above him and sing;
the star leads the magi. At his death, the sun is obscured
and is wrapped in darkness, the stones dash together, the
veil is torn, and the tombs are opened. At his resurrection,
there is an earthquake and the angels are present. When

he ascends into the heavens, the clouds embrace him. And when he returns in the future, the whole world will be shaken and the powers of the sky will be moved [Luke 2:9; Matt. 2:2; 27:51; 15:33; 28:2; Acts 1:9; Matt. 24:29]. Again, after the judgment there will be a great renewal, moving Isaiah in the thirtieth chapter [v. 16] to say that the moon will shine like the sun, and the sun itself will have a light seven times greater than it does now.

But is there any injury done to creation, given that it is vexed so because of the sins of mankind without any fault of its own? Chrysostom responds that there is no injury. For, he says, if they were made for my sake, no injustice can happen if they suffer because of me. Second, he adds that we must not transfer the notion of fairness and injustice to inanimate things lacking reason. Last, if they are afflicted because of us, when we achieve our blessed state, they will be restored with us.[6] Chrysostom also in his twenty-second homily on Genesis explains plainly that it is not unjust or absurd if creation is compelled to endure some calamities because of human beings. Should someone incur the wrath of a king, he says, not only does he himself receive punishment, but likewise his whole family experiences the burden. Mankind because of sin became subject to the curse and the wrath of God. Therefore, it is no wonder if all creation, which belongs to mankind's family, groans and suffers with it. Furthermore, he adduces from the Scriptures that all creation was submerged in the flood [Gen. 7:31]; in Sodom everything was consumed in the fire engulfing the wicked [Gen. 19:25]; in Egypt, be-

---

6. Chrysostom, *Homilia in Genesim* 22.17 (*Homilies on Genesis 18–45*, 81).

cause of Pharaoh's obstinacy, all creatures were destroyed [Exod. 14:28]. And in the book *Restoring the Fallen, to Theodorus*,[7] Chrysostom shows that after the day of judgment all things will be renewed, because the glory of the Lord will be manifest, filling and occupying all things. The Greek scholia also recognize the personification in the passage, as we do, and thus they assert that creation will be freed from the enslavement of corruption, because on our account it was made subject to corruption. Moreover, they show that the adoption of the sons of God will be revealed, because now the sons of God dwell among the sons of the devil and cannot easily be distinguished from them. However, our glory will be revealed in its time. Not only will it be apparent, but it will also be handed over; we have it in the present, but it is not yet full and perfect. But at that time, it will be completely released to us, and whatever is lacking now, we will have it in our possession.

---

7. Vermigli has in mind *De reparatione lapsi vel Paraeneses ad Theo-dorum lapsum* 13 (*An Exhortation to Theodore after His Fall*, NPNF, 9:142).

SELECT BIBLIOGRAPHY

The following entries are either cited in the introduction or translation, or they provide historical context to the theological debate concerning original sin.

PRIMARY

Ambrose. *Hexameron, Paradise*. New York: Fathers of the Church, Inc., 1961.

Anselm. *The Major Works*. Edited by Brian Davies and G. R. Evans. Oxford: Oxford University Press, 1998.

Augustine. *Against Julian the Pelagian*. Translated by Matthew Schumacher. New York: Fathers of the Church, 1957.

—————. *The Literal Meaning of Genesis*. Vol. 1, bks 1–6. Translated by John Hammond Taylor. New York: Paulist Press, 1982.

—————. *Questions on the Heptateuch*. In *The Works of St. Augustine: A Translation for the 21st Century*, translated by Joseph T. Leinhard, SJ, and Sean Doyle. New York: Augustinian Heritage Institute, 2016.

—————. *Saint Augustin: Anti-Pelagian Writings*. Translated by Peter Holmes, Robert Wallis, and Benjamin Warfield. 1st ser., vol. 5 of *Nicene and Post-Nicene Fathers*, edited by Philip Schaff. Grand Rapids, MI: Eerdmans, 1980 reprint.

—————. *To Simplician, on various questions*. In *Augustine: Earlier Writings*, translated and edited by John H. S.

Burleigh, 376–406. Philadelphia: The Westminster Press, 1953.

Basil of Caesarea, *St. Basil the Great: On the Human Condition*. Translated by Nonna Verna Harrison. Crestwood, NY: St. Vladimir's Seminary Press, 2005.

Calvin, John. *The Bondage and Liberation of the Will: A Defence of the Orthodox Doctrine of Human Choice against Pighius*. Edited by A. N. S. Lane. Translated by G. I. Davies. Grand Rapids, MI: Baker Books, 1996.

———. *Institutes of the Christian Religion*. Translated by Ford Lewis Battles. Atlanta: John Knox Press, 1975.

Chrysostom. *Homilies on Genesis 1–17*. Translated by Robert C. Hill. Washington, D.C.: The Catholic University of America Press, 1986.

———. *Homilies on Genesis 18–45*. Translated by Robert C. Hill. Washington, D.C.: The Catholic University of America Press, 1990.

Cyprian. *The Letters of Cyprian*. Vol. 3, Letters 55–66. Translated by G. W. Clarke. New York: Paulist Press, 1986.

Daneau, Lambert. *D. Aurelii Augustini Hiponensis Episcopi liber De haeresibus, ad Quodvultdeum . . . emendatus et commentariis illustratus, a quo eodem additae sunt haereses ab orbe condito ad constitutum Papismum et Mahumetismum, etiam ea quae hic erant ab Augustino praetermissae*. Geneva: Eustache Vignon, 1578.

Hugo of St. Victor. *On the Sacraments of the Christian Faith.* Translated by Roy Deferrari. College Station, PA: Penn State University Press, 1951.

Jerome. *Commentaries on the Twelve Prophets.* Translated by Thomas Scheck. Downers Grove, IL: InterVarsity Press, 2016.

Lombard, Peter. *The Sentences.* Translated by Guilio Silano. Toronto: Pontifical Institute of Medieval Studies, 2008.

Origen. *Commentary on the Epistle to the Romans.* Translated by Thomas Scheck. Washington, D.C.: The Catholic University of America Press, 2002.

Pighius, Albert. *De libero hominis arbitrio et divina gratia, Libri decem.* Cologne: Melchior Novesianus, 1542.

———. "De peccato originis controversia." In *Controversiarum praecipuarum in comitiis Ratisponensibus tractatarum et quibus nunc potissimum exagitatur Christi fides et religio, diligens, et luculenta explicatio.* Cologne: Melchior Novesianus, 1542, fols. ir-xxixr.

Vermigli, Peter Martyr. *In Epistolam S. Pauli Apostoli ad Romanos.* Zurich: [A. Gesner], 1559.

SECONDARY

Anderson, Marvin W. *Peter Martyr: A Reformer in Exile (1542–1562).* Nieuwkoop: B. de Graaf, 1975.

———. "Peter Martyr on Romans." *Scottish Journal of Theology* 26, no. 4 (1973): 401–20.

Backus, Irena and Aza Goudriaan. "*Semipelagianism*: The Origins of the Term and Its Passage into the History of Heresy." *Journal of Ecclesiastical History* 65, no. 1 (2014): 25–46.

Baschera, Luca. "Aristotle and Scholasticism." In *A Companion to Peter Martyr Vermigli*, edited by Torrance Kirby, Emidio Campi, and Frank James III, 133–60. Leiden: Brill, 2009.

———. "Peter Martyr Vermigli on Free Will: The Aristotelian Heritage of Reformed Theology." *Calvin Theological Journal* 42, no. 2 (2007): 325–46.

Beatrice, Pier Franco. *The Transmission of Sin: Augustine and the Pre-Augustinian Sources*. Translated by Adam Kamesar. Oxford: Oxford University Press, 2013.

Brady, Jules M. "St. Augustine's Theory of Seminal Reasons." *New Scholasticism* 38, no. 2 (1964): 141–58.

Campi, Emidio. "Genesis Commentary: Interpreting Creation." In *A Companion to Peter Martyr Vermigli*, edited by Torrance Kirby, Emidio Campi, and Frank James III, 209–30. Leiden: Brill, 2009.

Colish, Marcia. *Faith, Fiction, and Force in Medieval Baptismal Debates*. Washington, D.C.: The Catholic University of America Press, 2014.

Denlinger, Aaron. "Calvin's Understanding of Adam's Relationship to His Posterity: Recent Assertions of the Reformer's 'Federalism' Evaluated." *Calvin Theological Journal* 44, no. 2 (2009): 226–50.

Di Gangi, Mariano. *Peter Martyr Vermigli, 1499–1562: Renaissance Man, Reformation Master.* Lanham, MD: University Press of America, 1993.

Donnelly, John Patrick, SJ. *Calvinism and Scholasticism in Vermigli's Doctrine of Man and Grace.* Leiden: Brill, 1976.

————. "Peter Martyr on Fallen Man: A Protestant Scholastic View." PhD thesis, The University of Wisconsin-Madison, 1972.

Donnelly, John Patrick, SJ, Robert Kingdon, and Marvin Anderson. *A Bibliography of the Works of Peter Martyr Vermigli.* Ann Arbor, MI: Edwards Brothers, 1990.

Evans, Robert. *Pelagius: Inquiries and Reappraisals.* New York: The Seabury Press, 1968.

Faber, Jelle. "Imago Dei in Calvin: Calvin's Doctrine of Man as the Image of God in Connection with Sin and Restoration." In *Essays in Reformed Doctrine,* 227–50. Neerlandia, Alberta, Canada: Inheritance Publications, 1990.

Fedwick, Paul. *Basil of Caesarea: Christian, Humanist, Ascetic.* Toronto: Pontifical Institute of Mediaeval Studies, 1981.

Gousmett, Chris. "Creation Order and Miracle according to Augustine." *Evangelical Quarterly* 60, no. 3 (1988): 217–40.

Gross, Julius. *Geschichte des Erbsündendogmas: Ein Beitrag zur Geschichte des Problems vom Ursprung des Übels.* 4 vols. Munich: Ernst Reinhardt Verlag, 1960–72.

James, Frank III. "The Complex of Justification: Peter Martyr Vermigli versus Albert Pighius." In *Peter Martyr Vermigli: Humanism, Republicanism, Reformation*, edited by Emidio Campi, Frank James, and Peter Opitz, 45–58. Geneva: Droz, 2002.

Keech, Dominic. *The Anti-Pelagian Christology of Augustine of Hippo*. Oxford: Oxford University Press, 2012.

Landgraf, Artur Michael. "Die Vererbung der Sünden der Eltern auf die Kinder nach der Lehre des 12. Jahrhunderts." *Gregorianum* 21 (1940): 203–47.

Lane, Anthony. "Albert Pighius's Controversial Work on Original Sin." *Reformation and Renaissance Review* 4, no. 1 (2002): 29–61.

McLelland, Joseph C. "A Literary History of the *Loci communes*." In *A Companion to Peter Martyr Vermigli*, edited by Torrance Kirby, Emidio Campi, and Frank James III, 479–94. Leiden: Brill, 2009.

———. "Peter Martyr Vermigli: Scholastic or Humanist?" In *Peter Martyr Vermigli and Italian Reform*, edited by Joseph C. McLelland, 141–51. Waterloo, Ontario: Sir Wilfred Laurier University Press, 1980.

Pitkin, Barbara. "Nothing but Concupiscence: Calvin's Understanding of Sin and the *Via Augustini*." *Calvin Theological Journal* 34, no. 2 (1999): 347–69.

Rees, Brinley. *Pelagius: A Reluctant Heretic*. Wolfeboro, NH: The Boydell Press, 1988.

Steinmetz, David. "Peter Martyr Vermigli (1499–1562): The Eucharistic Sacrifice." In *Reformers in the Wings*, 151–61. Philadelphia: Fortress Press, 1971.

Strohm, Christoph. "Petrus Martyr Vermiglis *Loci communes* und Calvins *Institutio Christianae religionis*." In *A Companion to Peter Martyr Vermigli*, edited by Torrance Kirby, Emidio Campi, and Frank James III, 77–104. Leiden: Brill, 2009.

Vasoli, Cesare. "*Loci communes* and the Rhetorical and Dialectical Traditions." In *Peter Martyr Vermigli and Italian Reform*, edited by Joseph C. McLelland, 17–28. Waterloo, Ontario: Sir Wilfred Laurier University Press, 1980.

Vorster, Nico. "Calvin's Modification of Augustine's Doctrine of Original Sin." In *Restoration through Redemption: John Calvin Revisited*, edited by Henk Belt, 45–61. Leiden: Brill, 2013.

Widengren, Geo. *Mani and Manichaeism*. New York: Holt, Rinehart, and Winston, 1965.

Williams, N. P. *The Ideas of the Fall and of Original Sin: A Historical and Critical Study*. London: Longmans, Green and Co., Ltd., 1927.

INDEX

A

Abraham, 4, 10, 81, 98, 121–22, 132

Adam, xi, xv–xvi, xviii–xxii, xxiv, xxvi–xxix, 1, 4, 8n2, 13–18, 24, 26, 28, 32–35, 38, 39, 48, 49, 57, 59, 61, 66, 74, 78, 80, 81, 85, 101, 106, 113–15, 120, 124, 126, 127, 141

   and Christ, xvi, xix, xxviii, 57, 78, 80, 115, 126

   and Eve. *See* Eve

affection(s), xx, xxi, 14, 18, 21, 22, 26–27, 36, 48, 50, 53, 74, 116

Ambler, Wayne, 22n3

Ambrose, 58–59, 81, 111, 128, 134, 139–41

Anabaptists, xviii, 1

Anderson, Marvin, xxxin15

angels, xxix–xxx, 132, 135–38, 141, 143

Anselm, 2n1, 38, 39n8, 40, 47, 73

Aristotle, in1, ii, iii, iv, viii, 22, 48n6, 60n14, 79n4, 114

atheists, 138

Augustine, x, xin2, xii–xv, xxi, xxii, xxv, xvi, xxviii, xxxi, 3n3, 8, 10–11, 13n2, 14n3, 19, 21, 26–29, 34–38, 41, 44, 45–50, 53, 54, 56, 57–60, 61, 62, 63, 65, 73–74, 83, 84, 90–91, 94, 98, 101, 103, 107, 115, 117, 119–23, 125, 126, 132, 133, 134, 141

B

Backus, Irena, xviiin8

corruption, human, xiii, xix–xxii, xxv–xxvi, xxviii–xxix,
    xxx, 1, 3n3, 10, 11, 15, 18, 22–29, 31, 32, 35,
    36, 38, 40 43, 45, 48–49, 50, 53–54, 55, 63,
    66–67, 69, 74, 75, 77–79, 82, 90, 91,
    94, 97, 100, 102, 104, 105, 110–11, 113, 116,
    117, 124, 125, 132, 136, 137, 145.
    See also concupiscence
Cranmer, Thomas, vi
creation (act), xviii, 13n1, 58, 60, 74, 75, 121, 123, 139
    of humans, xix, xxi, xxii, xxiv, xxixn13, 9 , 17, 18,
    36, 38, 40, 43–44, 45, 49–50, 55, 58, 61, 67,
    75, 78, 79, 102, 113, 120
    of soul, xiii, xxix, 2, 74, 76–77, 79, 119–121, 123,
    124
creation (creatures), xx, xxii, xxix–xxx, 28n9, 44, 55, 79,
    131–145
    groaning of, 56, 132–35, 139–40, 142, 144–45
Cyprian, 57

D
damnation, xii, xvii, 14, 33, 47–48, 39, 63, 91, 124, 129
Daneau, Lambert, xiv–xix, xxv
de Félice, Paul, xivn5
Denlinger, Aaron, 38n7
depravity, xxii, xxviii, xxix, 4, 15, 18, 21–22, 25, 26,
    31n1, 36, 45, 54, 66, 70, 71, 105, 110,
    113, 116, 125
descendants. *See* posterity. *See also* child(ren)
devil, 10–11, 23, 56, 57, 64, 114–115, 145
disease, xxix, xxvi, 11, 27, 39, 48, 60, 85, 121, 125, 131
Donnelly, John Patrick, iin4, xin1, xxxin15

E

Egypt, plagues, 139, 144–45

election. *See* predestination

elements, 3

Epicureans, 138

Evans, Robert, xiin3

Eve, xi, xix, xxii, 60, 113–115, 120, 128

evil (sin), xii, xxi, xxiii–xxiv, xxv, xxx, 1, 3n4, 4, 9, 15,
        23–24, 25, 27, 34, 36, 45, 55, 56, 58, 60, 62,
        66, 74–76, 78, 79, 90, 94, 104–105, 106, 110,
        118, 124, 136, 140, 141, 142

F

Fall, xi, xiin3, xvi, xix, xxivn12, xxvi, xxvii, xxix, 1, 4, 31,
        47, 57n5, 67n2, 127

fathers, sins of the. *See* posterity, and sins of the fathers

Fatio, Olivier, xivn5

Fenlon, Dermot, iiin6

flesh, xxv, xxvi, 1, 3, 4, 7–9, 14, 21, 23, 26–27, 38, 46,
        48, 51–54, 55, 57, 73, 74, 98, 101, 103, 104,
        105, 116, 120, 125
   and spirit, xxii, 21, 52, 54, 105
   and Spirit, 51–52

flood, 24, 86, 138, 144

G

generations. *See* posterity, and sins of the fathers

gifts, divine/celestial, xix, xxii, xxiv–xxv, xxvii, xxixn13,
        14n4, 17, 31, 39, 47, 62, 65, 66–67, 76, 105

Goudriaan, Aza, xviiin8

Gousmett, Chris, 28n9

M

MacCulloch, Diarmaid, ix–x
Manicheans, xxiii–xxiv, 60, 133
marriage, xiv, xvi, xviii, xxvii, 2, 79, 97, 98, 120, 124
Mary, virgin, xxix, 122
Masson, Robert, vii
McLelland, Joseph, viiin16, ix, xnn22–23
McNair, Philip, iin4, iiin5, iv, v
Melchizedek, 121–22
Millett, Paul, 24n3

N

Neo-platonists, 28n9
new man, xiii, 43, 53
newborn. *See* infant(s)

O

offspring. *See* posterity
old man, 7, 50, 53, 82
Origen, 61, 142

P

Pelagius, Pelagians, xii–xx, xxii–xxiv, xxvi–xxviii, 1–4,
    10–11, 34–35, 36, 37, 47, 59–63, 65–66, 83,
    85, 101, 115, 117, 123, 125, 127
philosophers, xxv, 3n4, 28, 36, 45, 102
Pighius, Albert, xii–xiii, xvii–xviii, xx–xxi, xxii–xxiv,
    xxviii, 2n1, 3n2, 3n4, 13–19, 21–29, 32–33,
    35–41, 46–47, 48, 50–52, 63–64, 65–67,
    69–70, 73, 74–75, 80, 83, 88n1, 91, 102

S

salvation, i, vii, xvi, xvii, 17, 27, 34, 35, 51, 77–78, 79, 81, 83, 84, 91, 99, 100, 117, 118, 134, 140, 141

schoolmen, iv, xiii, 26–27, 28, 41, 54, 67, 74, 79, 83, 103, 106–7, 123

Scotus, Duns, 54

seed (procreation), xviii, xxiii, xxv, 5, 57, 59, 69, 74–75, 80–81, 97, 101, 119, 120

seed (offspring). *See* posterity

seminal reason, 28, 74

seminal structure, preexisting, 121

servant, servitude, xxx, 16–17, 22, 25–26, 131, 132, 137, 139, 140, 142, 143

sex, xxv, 28, 124. *See also* procreation

sickness. *See* disease

Simler, Josiah, iin3, iiinn7–8, iv–v, vii

sin(s), viin15, xi, xviii, xix–xxiii, xxv, xxvii–xxviii, 2, 3–4, 7–12, 13, 14, 15–19, 21–22, 23n4, 24–25, 29, 30, 31–33, 34–40, 45, 47–54, 57–63, 65–66, 69n1, 73–82, 85–86, 88–96, 97–98, 100, 101–8, 109–11, 113–18, 123–29, 131, 135, 139, 140, 141, 143, 144

actual, xx, xxv, xxviii, 3, 13, 37, 45, 63, 83n1, 84, 100, 103, 116

of Adam, xi–xii, xv, xvi, xviii, xix–xxii, xxiv, xxx, 4, 10, 13–18, 23n4, 26, 28, 29, 30, 31–33, 57, 59, 61, 65–67, 73, 85, 106

noetic effects of, xxivn12

original, xi–xxx, xxxii, 1–4, 8–10, 13, 15–16, 22n2, 25, 26–29, 34–35, 37n6, 38, 45, 47–48, 53, 57n5, 60, 62–64, 65–67, 70–71, 73–82, 83–84,

MORE FROM DAVENANT PRESS

INTRODUCTION TO PROTESTANT THEOLOGY

- *Reformation Theology: A Reader of Primary Sources with Introductions*
- *Grace Worth Fighting For: Recapturing the Vision of God's Grace in the Canons of Dordt*

PETER MARTYR VERMIGLI LIBRARY

- *Dialogue on the Two Natures in Christ*
- *Philosophical Works: On the Relation of Philosophy to Theology*
- *The Oxford Treatise and Disputation on the Eucharist, 1549*
- *Predestination and Justification: Two Theological Loci*

VERMIGLI'S COMMON PLACES

- *On Original Sin (Vol. 1)*
- *On Free Will and the Law (Vol. 2)*

LIBRARY OF EARLY ENGLISH PROTESTANTISM

- *James Ussher and a Reformed Episcopal Church: Sermons and Treatises on Ecclesiology*
- *The Apology of the Church of England*
- *Jurisdiction Regal, Episcopal, Papal*
- *Radicalism: When Reform Becomes Revolution*
- *Divine Law and Human Nature*

- *The Word of God and the Words of Man*
- *In Defense of Reformed Catholic Worship*
- *A Learned Discourse on Justification*
- *The Laws of Ecclesiastical Polity: In Modern English, Vol. 1 (Preface–Book IV)*
- *The Shining Human Creature: Christian Ethics Vol. 1*
- *Made like the Maker: Christian Ethics Vol. 2*
- *A Treatise on Christian Moderation*
- *The Word Made Flesh: A Treatise on Christology and the Sacraments from Hooker's Laws*

DAVENANT GUIDES

- *Jesus and Pacifism: An Exegetical and Historical Investigation*
- *The Two Kingdoms: A Guide for the Perplexed*
- *Natural Law: A Brief Introduction and Biblical Defense*
- *Natural Theology: A Biblical and Historical Introduction and Defense*

AMERICAN THEOLOGY SERIES

- *Communicating God's Trinitarian Fullness: A Commentary on Jonathan Edwards' End for Which God Created the World*
- *Religion and Republic: Christian American from the Founding to the Civil War*

DAVENANT RETRIEVALS

- *A Protestant Christendom?*
  The World the Reformation Made

- *People of the Promise:*
  A Mere Protestant Ecclesiology

- *Philosophy and the Christian:*
  The Quest for Wisdom in the Light of Christ

- *The Lord Is One: Reclaiming Divine Simplicity*

CONVIVIUM PROCEEDINGS

- *For the Healing of the Nations: Essays on Creation,*
  Redemption, and Neo-Calvinism

- *For Law and for Liberty: Essays on the Legacy of*
  Protestant Political Thought

- *Beyond Calvin: Essays on the Diversity*
  of the Reformed Tradition

- *God of Our Fathers: Classical Theism*
  for the Contemporary Church

- *Reforming the Catholic Tradition:*
  The Whole Word for the Whole Church

- *Reforming Classical Education:*
  Toward A New Paradigm

OTHER PUBLICATIONS

- *Enduring Divine Absence:*
  The Challenge of Modern Atheism

- *Without Excuse: Scripture, Reason,*
  and Presuppositional Apologetics

- *Being A Pastor: Pastoral Treatises of John Wycliffe*
- *Serious Comedy: The Philosophical and Theological Significance of Tragic and Comic Writing in the Western Tradition*
- *Protestant Social Teaching: An Introduction*
- *Begotten or Made?*
- *Why Do Protestants Convert?*

ABOUT THE DAVENANT INSTITUTE

The Davenant Institute aims to retrieve the riches of classical Protestantism in order to renew and build up the contemporary church: building networks of friendship and collaboration among evangelical scholars committed to Protestant resourcement, publishing resources old and new, and offering training and discipleship for Christians thirsting after wisdom.

We are a nonprofit organization supported by your tax-deductible gifts. Learn more about us, and donate, at www.davenantinstitute.org.

Made in the USA
Monee, IL
15 September 2024

65830853R00125